Hot BARRELS!

Hot *BARRELS!*

Shooting Superstitions, Facts and Fallacies

JC Jeremy Hobson

Cartoons by **Bryn Parry**

Quiller

Copyright © J C Jeremy Hobson (text) 2017
Copyright © Bryn Parry (illustrations) 2017

First published in the UK in 2017 by
Quiller, an imprint of Quiller Publishing Ltd

British Library Cataloguing-in-Publication Data
A catalogue record for this book is available from
the British Library

ISBN 978 1 84689 246 2

Designed by Guy Callaby
Printed and bound in China

Quiller
An imprint of Quiller Publishing Ltd
Wykey House, Wykey, Shrewsbury SY4 1JA
Tel: 01939 261616 Fax: 01939 261606
E-mail: info@quillerbooks.com
Website: www.quillerpublishing.com

Contents

Acknowledgements

Firstly – and very definitely, most importantly, my utmost gratitude must go to Bryn Parry for agreeing to illustrate this humble tome ... it's an absolute honour to have his cartoons gracing its pages. As most will know, Bryn has been quite literally drawing from life (especially the shooting field) for many years and then, in 2007, he and his wife Emma founded the world-famous charity Help for Heroes (H4H), which has raised millions of pounds to provide direct, practical support for wounded, injured and sick service personnel, veterans and their loved ones.

Grateful thanks too to Quiller Publishing; not only for managing to persuade Bryn to agree to illustrating *Hot Barrels!*, but also for permission to use several extracts taken from *The Keen Countryman's Miscellany*, by Peter Holt. In addition, I've included two or three short extracts from some of my previously published books by Quiller; apologies if any faithful readers think they've read a particular account before – they probably have! Also, several inclusions have been taken from some of my previously published articles; in particular my regular weekly column in *Countryman's Weekly*. Thanks must therefore go to all those involved for their kindness in allowing their reproduction here.

The account of crowing pheasants and the North Sea battle, originally published in the *Manchester Guardian* of February 1915, is by courtesy of Guardian News & Media Limited. Other sources and references are mentioned throughout the text and are also included in 'Bibliography, Further Reading, References and Sources'.

In connection with the above, I have drawn much information and inspiration from various articles and letters in shooting magazines, books and

internet forums – a great deal of which is either out of copyright, is in the public domain, or available for what would normally be considered 'fair use'. Therefore, in accordance with my understanding of the UK's copyright laws, I have not necessarily sought permission to quote very minor extracts taken from book, magazine and internet – but can assure anyone concerned that I have not taken any quote and used it out of context ... or to the detriment of what was intended by the author. In instances where more than a few words have been used, every reasonable effort has been made to contact possible copyright owners. Should any that I have been so far unable to trace happen to read this, I would be delighted if they would get in touch with the publishers in order that the omission can be rectified in any future reprints.

J.C. Jeremy Hobson
Hampshire
May 2017

Preface

There's much tradition in all field sports – and that's exactly as it should be. Field sports in general, and game shooting and gamekeeping in particular, seem to have more than their fair share so it would be very surprising if, over the generations, word of mouth hadn't created long-held 'facts' that have been repeated unquestioned during conversations wherever and whenever like-minded shooting enthusiasts gather.

Of some there can be no doubt and what an aged relative told you fifty years ago might well remain pretty much the same half a century on. Others are, though, somewhat more suspect and, if explored more thoroughly, wouldn't stand up to much scrutiny; indeed they might almost be classed as superstition, particularly, it would seem, when it comes to how some Guns approach a shooting day!

Quiet times out in the field, in a butt whilst waiting for the first grouse to come tantalisingly forward, on a peg in readiness for a pheasant to rocket over the valley, or standing expectantly in the hope that a partridge will flip fast and furious over the hedgerow, are all times for reflection and careful observation of what surrounds you – and then, when that first bird arrives and you kill it stone dead with a single shot, you might wonder at exactly what speed it was travelling.

A clean shot like that might make you consider 'bragging rights' – traditionally frowned upon by the serious sportsman and woman. As Robert Jarman, contributing to *The Gentleman's Journal* in December 2012, commented: '[The] serious shooting man … is there for the sport and the craic, not to count his personal tally after each drive ... There is nothing more unbecoming that a Gun 'blowing his own trumpet' and it is far more satisfying for your neighbour to come up and say; 'you shot very well on that last drive'. Despite that undeniable truth, there are, though, the odd occasions – as we shall see – when certain 'bragging rights' might be permitted!

While some are happy to unquestionably quote what they've heard as 'gospel', others are far more pedantic – which may or may not be a good thing. For instance, when, on a BBC television cookery programme, a judge told his co-judges that he could taste that it was a 'grey-legged' partridge ... and that it came from its native country of Norfolk – it was an exchange of pure drivel that annoyed me for the rest of the evening. There are, as we all know, either 'grey' (English) partridges or 'red-legged' (French) partridges, but there never has been a 'grey-legged' variety ... also, no matter how fine his taste buds, there's no way in the world that the judging 'celebrity' could ever tell exactly from what county in England his particular bird on a plate had originated. Other viewers would, I'm sure, have accepted what the man said and it's by such means that fallacies soon become 'facts'.

I am, I must admit, an enthusiastic user of social media, especially Twitter. I 'follow' and am 'followed' by a variety of people with a multitude of opinions. A difference of opinion is stimulating; particularly when there are accurate facts to hand upon which the 'tweeter' has formed his or her judgment. Occasionally, though, some of the Twitterati 'retweet' propaganda from the likes of the League Against Cruel Sports (LACS) without first of all checking their facts. How can it be, for example, that, as recently stated in a campaign to

ban the legitimate use of snares, the numbers of badgers supposedly accidentally trapped and killed annually in wires intended for fox control amounted to (according to Defra figures) exactly the whole badger population of Great Britain? If that were true then there'd obviously not be a badger left – which, as most are aware, is, quite patently, not the case. As Charles Spurgeon, nineteenth century Baptist preacher, is quoted as saying: 'A lie can travel half way around the world while the truth is putting on its shoes.'

With Spurgeon's words in mind (and written well before the age of social media, therefore extremely prescient), I thought it prudent to include a chapter entitled 'What the Papers Say'. Information is occasionally referred to as a 'factoid', however, no matter what you may think from the name, it's not actually a 'fact' at all – more something that has been repeated so often (particularly in journalism) that people nowadays accept it as being the truth.

According to *Wikipedia*, 'The term factoid can in common usage mean either a false or spurious statement presented as a fact, as well as according to [both *Webster's* and the *Oxford English Dictionary*] a true, if brief or trivial item of news or information.' Thought to have been first used by Norman Mailer, in his 1973 biography of Marilyn Monroe (or is that just another 'factoid'?), he reckoned that they were 'facts which have no existence before appearing in a magazine or newspaper'. *The Washington Times* has since further opined that a factoid is: 'something that looks like a fact, could be a fact, but in fact is not a fact'!

It is then, important to sort the 'wheat from the chaff' and where possible, impart relevant, accurate information. There is, though, time for levity; some snippets from contemporary newspapers are included and will, on occasion, cause the reader a wry smile or bemused expression regarding their credibility.

Superstition, an observation of nature and weather conditions, the speed of a particular bird, bragging rights, the best way of bathing your dog (!), the perceived romance of poaching and the various ways in which it is carried out, the correct ways to use an ordnance survey map or satnav to aid you to your shooting destination and much, much more are all given due credence, debunked, scientifically proven or left deliberately hanging in the breeze for fear of losing some of the mystery. Whilst it's appropriate to bring some things 'bang-up-to-date' and to talk of research, changing attitudes and knowledge, there are times when it's undoubtedly better for some of the mystique to remain!

In *Hot Barrels!*, I hope to provide some definite answers, both from my own observations and the experiences of others, and to add unquestionable results from impeccable scientific research so as to provide a light-hearted, quirky tome to be enjoyed by the seasonal fireside with a drink to hand and a sporting dog at foot. However, as solitary an occupation reading might be (akin to wildfowling or pigeon shooting perhaps), the information thus gleaned might well be shared around the shoot lunch table, or whilst sitting on a bale in a barn eating sandwiches, for – as any true shooting person can confirm – the real pleasures come from sharing life (and knowledge) with kindred spirits. Talking of which, 'spirits' of the unworldly nature haven't been forgotten either, and mention of them can be found at the end of Chapter 12: 'Sporting Domesticity'!

Guns and
Shooting Days

There's a lot of ritual attached to shoot day preparation, much of it based on practicalities – although there are those who prepare in a certain way because of their own self-imposed superstitions!

From the practical point of view it makes sense to lay out as much of your clothing and equipment as you can the night before as then there's less chance you'll forget anything due to a last-minute rush. Some can even be packed in the car in readiness but, in the interest of safety, that obviously doesn't include one's shotgun or rifle. Sporting dogs may also influence how much you can prepare ahead of time as, for many, just as soon as they see everything being gathered together, they tend to become extremely excitable and vocal!

A checklist is always a good idea and, once you have perfected it, it may pay to get it laminated for longevity and place it somewhere near the back door or, if you are fortunate enough to own one, in the gun room.

Small items such as dog leads, dog whistle, spare ear defenders, anti-midge spray (for those August days on grouse or late summer forays after pigeon), sunglasses and a towelling cravat to keep the rain from running down your neck can all be kept together in a small game bag or fishing bag used solely for this purpose. In that way, you are only carrying one thing out to the car rather than a handful of relatively small, easily misplaced items.

ONCE FORGOTTEN ...

Lots of people have forgotten guns — and on occasion, gun dogs. Some have even taken the wrong dogs home with them. This story was told quite recently: 'A Gun and a picker-up on our shoot both had black Labradors. Each drove about 30 miles home (in opposite directions) and, on going to let their dogs out of the back of their respective vehicles, couldn't understand why the dogs just sat there looking at them.' Seemingly, the wrong dogs had been taken and a return trip to the shoot venue was necessary in order to reunite the right dogs with the right owners.

Anecdotes abound as to what people have forgotten or mislaid prior to a shooting day — some are apocryphal and some retold as rural myths ... others, such as these, are absolutely true!

Once drove from Edinburgh down to the borders to shoot; we had a coffee before we started and it was only then that I realised that my comfy footwear were my slippers — and I'd forgotten my boots. Luckily, a fellow Gun was able to help out with a spare pair.

I was once loading and, after getting cartridges, bags and gun slips out of 'my' Gun's car, asked him where his gun was — he went as white as a sheet ... and it turned out that he'd put it in his son's car some 150 miles away.

On another occasion, I pulled the Gun's gun from its slip on the first drive — only to discover it was a rifle ... he'd been stalking the evening before and forgotten to change guns.

CHECK LIST
GUN
SQUIBS
CERTIFICATE
BOOTS
EAR DEFENDERS
TIE
TIP
WHISTLE
DOG FOOD
LEAD
STICK

A checklist is always a good idea

I remember a stalker I was out with being somewhat peeved about his client the day before not turning up. When he contacted him, the stalker apologised profusely, saying; 'I knew we were supposed to meet at Abersomething, so I went to Aberfeldy' ... he was so nearly right ... he should have gone to Aberfoyle.

DON'T BE LATE!

Today, satellite navigation can get us to the meeting point for a day's shooting (even so, it seems that some people manage to be continually late on such occasions), but it wasn't all that long ago when all we had to rely on were maps and verbal directions. Nevertheless, even the most modern technology doesn't always include the out-of-the-way places sometimes chosen as a meeting point for a shooting day, hunt meet or stalking foray and it's often necessary to resort to old-fashioned mapping skills. Yet, somewhat worryingly, according to research carried out by the RAC Direct Insurance, half of today's young drivers don't know how to read a road atlas.

The RAC results suggest a growing dependence on digital technology is to blame for poor map reading and say that road maps are becoming increasingly redundant, with more than one in ten (14 per cent) drivers admitting to never using one. This figure rises to one in five (20 per cent) drivers aged under thirty-five, whilst more than a quarter (26 per cent) of this same age group don't even carry a road map in their vehicle.

Where am I?

In remote and difficult terrain such as is occasionally encountered out shooting or stalking, it might be advisable to plan ahead and acquaint oneself with a map of the area. As an Ordnance Survey download, *Advanced Map Reading*, points out:

> Interpreting the shape of the land on a map using contour lines is an extremely useful navigational tool. Looking at the lines and creating a mental picture of the landscape will allow you to plan ... effectively. Orange or brown contour lines on maps join points of equal height above sea level together, and are usually measured in 5- or 10-metre height intervals. One of the easiest ways to convert contour lines into a mental picture is to imagine the lines as high tide marks left by the sea. As the water level drops it leaves a line every 5 or 10 metres on the landscape, forming the contour lines.

It is, however, well worth knowing that smaller features may be missed by contour lines. If a feature is 9m high on the land it may not appear on a map with contour lines at 10m intervals — which can be very confusing when you see the actual landscape and it contains features you haven't imagined because they don't appear on your map! The Ordnance Survey download further mentions that:

> When interpreting contour lines you can use symbols and features around them to get a better understanding of how the landscape will appear in reality. In particular, you should look for the symbols for cliffs, outcrops, scree and streams, as they will give you a valuable insight into the formation of a landscape.

A BRIDGE TOO FAR?

En route to the shoot, satnav or an Ordnance Survey map may well take you under a bridge. Particularly superstitious travellers are sometimes known to touch the roof of their car – a gesture seemingly intended to hold up the bridge as one passes underneath. Should you feel the need to do so whilst driving, it's probably not a good idea to use both hands as, letting go of the steering wheel entirely is far more likely to create disastrous consequences!

Parting is such sweet sorrow

Smaller bridges may be encountered actually on the shoot itself – and they are not without consequence if of a suspicious, superstitious mind. At the end of the day, never say goodbye to a friend whilst actually standing on a bridge for to do so means you are unlikely to see them again. Why? A bridge, by its very nature is suspended between two pieces of land and saying goodbye on a bridge indicates separation.

Building bridges

New footbridges are often built on the grouse moor or lowland shoot. Although they are likely to have already been traversed by the keeper, estate maintenance staff, or agricultural contractors whilst being built, it may be just as well to check as it's considered bad luck to be the first across a new bridge no matter what its size, where it spans or in whatever location. Doing so is supposed to anger the Devil who, or so we are led to believe, is incapable of building such a structure. To counteract his anger, some bridge builders traditionally leave a small amount of money tucked in the stones, concrete or wooden beams used in its construction.

If you are unsure as to whether or not a new bridge has been previously trod, you could always send your dog across first as a preventative measure – animals are supposedly exempt from the wrath of the Devil in this particular instance!

SERIOUSLY SUPERSTITIOUS

There are many Guns and keepers who are somewhat suspicious about what to wear and how to behave on a shooting day.

- One particular individual always has to wear red socks with blue flashes – and put his left boot on first. Another apparently wears certain ties on certain days (but doesn't disclose how he arrives at a decision).

- A surprising number of people seemingly insist on starting out a day's shooting with an uneven amount of cartridges or bullets.

- In the world of clay-shooting, some even go to the trouble of turning their cartridges so you can read the manufacturer's name the right way up in both barrels.

- Some Guns like to start and end their game season/shooting day with a successful shot – and think it a bad omen if they don't.

Science of the occult!

There's even more shooting superstition to be found in the 1903 book, *Encyclopaedia of Superstitions, Folklore and the Occult Science of the World*, which includes these little gems:

- Save whatever shot you find in the first wild duck you pick in the autumn; it will bring you good luck.
- For the guns of two hunters to accidentally strike together when out hunting, it is a sign they will be together next year.
- If you count the bullets before you start out shooting, you will have bad luck.
- If you drop a shot [cartridge] whilst loading a gun, that is your lucky shot.
- If a woman touches a gun, it will not shoot straight (that, apparently from the Turks Islands).
- A gun will shoot straight if rubbed with the fat of a corpse (seemingly, an Irish superstition ... but the saying doesn't stipulate whether the corpse be animal or human!)

Other random superstitions and observations collated from Guns around the UK include:

- Both cartridges have to be the same colour (although brand/shot size are less important).

- If I don't connect with my first two shots, the rest of the day's shooting will be a wash-out.

- If I don't fire a shot on the first drive, my shooting will be dreadful for the rest of the day.

- I shot very well once using a cartridge belt, so now I have to fill up my belt with cartridges from my bag every drive and shoot with the belt on!

- I have to eat porridge every morning I go shooting ...

BANG, BANG, BUGGER ...

Most of us miss a bird from time to time (some more than others ... and I very much include myself here) For most, there's a reason for the odd 'blip' but when such things become more frequent, it's usually put down to getting older and thereby naturally failing eyesight. It's a commonly brought out excuse, but is there any need to put up with the myth and just accept things as they are? Those in the know think not — and suggest the following: 'If your form changes, first check for any changes in your eye dominance.' Also, and it's quite obvious really: 'If you've not had an eye-check recently, do so ... correcting clarity and a sharpness of vision can often be achieved with glasses, contact lenses or laser surgery.'

I LOVE TO GO A'WANDERING ...

It's long been supposed that some strains/breeds of pheasant (often put down on a low-lying estate in the hope of producing better, more sporting 'high fliers') tend to wander more than others — but is there any truth in this? Many keepers will say there is and, way back in February 1999, a correspondent to the *Shooting Gazette*'s Letters page seemed to confirm their thinking:

> We have always released 'normal' pheasants as we considered the new strains of Scandinavian and Michigan bluebacks unnecessary on our undulating ground and wooded valleys and have never had any straying problems.
>
> Last season a proportion of our 'normal' pheasants turned out to be Michigan bluebacks.
>
> The result was some excellent shooting for our neighbours! One of their woods over 1.5 miles away returned over 60 of our Michigan cock pheasants.
>
> We had our worst returns ever and a very frustrating year for the keeper, who was at his wits end.

THE COURT JESTER

No matter whether your shooting is walked up or driven, one thing that remains constant throughout is the camaraderie such sport engenders amongst all its participants. Whenever any group of like-minded people gather together, be they Guns, beaters, pickers-up or indeed anyone connected with the day, you can be sure that, even if they've never met each other before that morning, by lunchtime they will be laughing and joking as if they were lifelong friends.

Some friendly barracking is a part of every shooting day and at least one of the Guns ends up playing the court jester. Sometimes this takes the form of a few 'in' jokes; some very funny spontaneous repartee or harmless pranks. Dare to wear an unusual hat, overly bright shooting stockings, or a waistcoat seemingly made from your grandmother's curtains and you know you're heading for trouble ...!

HEALTH AND EFFICIENCY

Apparently the great nineteenth century sportsman, Colonel Peter Hawker, was ill, on and off, for most of his life. But, when all else failed; when he was 'trembling with ague' and 'sick as a dog', he'd put his gun under his arm and go out for a day's hard slog on the shooting field — claiming more than once how often he'd cheated his doctor of the 'five golden guineas' usually paid for a call-out charge and consultation.

Therefore, is the best treatment for 'man-flu' not bed, but fresh air and exercise — particularly that taken with dog and gun?

GRI(S)T TO THE MILL

There's a lot of conversation about grouse moor management that is given as fact whenever a group of like-minded Guns get together. Most will (correctly) pontificate on the need to have several stages of heather growth to provide nesting, brooding and feeding areas. Possibly less understood are the potential disease problems — particularly when it comes to the parasitic worm *Trichostrongylus tenuis* that, left unchecked, can decimate grouse moor stocks.

In an effort to combat the disease, medicated grit was developed — grouse use grit to grind up their food (mainly heather) — and, like Lily the Pink's Medicinal Compound (you have to be of a certain era to know about that one), has proved most efficacious in every case!

There are, though, worries as to its continued use. Almost all those directly connected with such things agree that it is absolutely essential that grouse should not be given access to medicated grit all year round. There are two main reasons: firstly, continued use could result in the worm species developing an immunity to the drug and, secondly, because of the medical formulation of the drug used, it is necessary for all birds entering the human food chain to have had no access to medicated grit for at least twenty-eight days previous – in effect then, twenty-eight days before the start of the shooting season on August 12th.

PACKING PARTRIDGES

Most know that grouse will 'pack' towards the end of the season, but what of wild coveys of grey partridges? Several theories abound – including that of one brood losing their parents and joining up with another. Others mention that it may be to do with a dry summer when, in the days when wild greys were far more plentiful, such packing, or joining together of coveys was more often noted during 'drought' conditions.

As a result of research, it's now known that coveys of young partridges will occasionally be joined by adult birds who have no chicks, or by a cock bird whose female has been killed but, even so, nowhere is there any mention of a dry summer making wild coveys more likely to join together.

By late December, most will be pairing up – as can be seen in the following 'Six Golden Rules for Game Shooters' as drawn up by the Game and Wildlife Conservation Trust (GWCT), who have carried out a monumental amount of work relating to creating the best natural conditions for wild partridge welfare and survival.

1. Do not shoot wild grey partridges if you have fewer than twenty birds per 250 acres (100 hectares) in the autumn. Below this level the population has little ability to compensate for shooting losses.

2. Stop shooting wild grey partridges as soon as the threshold of twenty birds per 250 acres (100 hectares) is reached, for the same reason.

3. Avoid shooting grey partridges after the end of December. Birds pair up in the New Year and shooting at this time reduces the breeding stock.

4. Never shoot at grey partridges that are in pairs.

5. With driven redleg or pheasant shooting, take special precautions to ensure that wild greys are not shot at the same time. Warn the Guns if grey partridges are likely to be on the drive. Tell the guns to watch out for higher birds in tight coveys that might be greys. Tell them, if in doubt, not to shoot. Perhaps fine them if they shoot greys! Arrange a system of whistles for beaters to warn guns that greys have been flushed – their distinctive call also helps to identify them. Have observers in the line of guns to do the same.

6. ***Do not shoot grey partridges at all unless you also take steps to conserve them.***

STOPPING AND STARTING

Frequently asked is the question, 'Should the partridge and pheasant shooting seasons start and finish later?'

As the law currently stands, the pheasant season in England, Wales and Scotland lasts from 1 October until 1 February; the partridge season runs from 1 September until 1 February, and wild duck and goose seasons are from 1 September until 31 January. Periodically, noises are made at the highest levels regarding the possibility of an extension to the game shooting season into February.

There are supporters both for and against: one typical response being: 'The quality of the birds is definitely better later in the season as they are more mature and wiser. Plus, the poorer ones have been harvested.' Another comments along similar lines: 'There may be strong arguments for an extension – particularly the economic benefits to the country and the growing market for game meat.' Others believe that there's 'little desire within the shooting community to extend the season. These dates are set for practical management and conservation reasons and must be considered alongside the interests of the countryside as a whole.'

POKE A SQUIRREL

Grey squirrels (rather than grey partridges as above) offer some interesting shooting once the game season is over and it's possible to go drey-poking before the leaves begin to unfurl, making the dreys difficult to see. It's good sport (and, because of the cartridge to kill ratio, the cartridge manufacturers love it too!) and it does everyone from farmer to woodman, to gamekeeper, a great service.

From being introduced to Britain in the Victorian era, the grey has, unfortunately, gone from strength to strength – and to the detriment of the native red squirrel. Keeping their numbers under control is an ongoing task and whilst drey-poking is, as we've already established, not the most effective method; it does, however, offer some interesting and often amusing opportunities. Over the years I've witnessed scenes more reminiscent of Fred Carno's Army when escaping squirrels scamper round the other side of the tree and the waiting Guns all dash round there to try and get a shot. Poking poles have also been dropped in a mad panic when a squirrel decides to try make his escape down the pole and towards the operator.

WHAT'S IN A NAME?

From a letter to the *Fieldsports* magazine's mailbag (April/May 2016):

… when I was at school in the 1950s, all activities such as football, rugby, cricket, hockey, tennis, badminton and the like were called games and were taught by a games teacher. The term sport related to shooting, fishing, hunting and falconry and had done so since medieval times.

'Blood' sports or 'field' sports?

Have you ever wondered when the term 'blood sports' was first used by the antis in connection with what might better and more fairly be described as 'field sports'? It's actually been in use longer than you might think – and was adopted by the Humanitarian League in the 1890s to condemn sports in which they considered, 'pleasure was obtained at the cost of suffering to animals'.

WHAT THE BLOODY HELL!

Occasionally one witnesses or sees a photo of a youngster being 'blooded' after having just shot his first game bird. Archaic and perhaps with not much place in the modern world (it certainly gives the 'antis' something to get excited about!), it is, however, traditional to wipe the merest smear of blood on the cheeks or forehead of one who has killed his first bird or, in hunting circles (before the Hunting Act), when the newcomer first witnessed hounds account for their quarry.

Or is it? According to some, 'blooding' the tyro should traditionally only be applied to field sports where deer are involved and is not applicable at all to the killing of other birds or animals.

St Hubert, the patron saint of hunting, was born in France in the seventh century. Keen on hunting from an early age, he was far less keen on going to church — a cardinal (forgive the pun!) sin in a Catholic country.

Out in the forests of the Ardennes on a Good Friday when all others were at church, Hubert's hounds raised a stag and hunted it until it was cornered.

Hubert dismounted and went towards it in readiness to administer the 'coup-de-grace'. As the animal turned to face him, Hubert noticed that, between its antlers was an illuminated crucifix (difficult not to notice, one would imagine!). A voice from above then told Hubert that, unless he reformed his ideas and went to church more often, he would end up in Hell when the time came for him to shuffle off his mortal coil. Understandably alarmed, Hubert went to seek advice from his local bishop; as a result of which he became a priest and eventually, the Bishop of Maastricht.

He was, however, not quite done with deer hunting. As is the case with many saints, Hubert performed several recorded miracles throughout his life; in addition to which, he was thought to be immune to rabies — a disease that was affecting humans and decimating several hound packs of the time. Hunting hound owners brought their hounds to church to have them blessed by Hubert and it was said that many were saved as a result — which is the reason that a St Hubert's Mass is held in some places even today; particularly in France where they are incorporated into the programme of many a 'fête de la chasse' or game fair.

In remembrance of Hubert, after he died in 727 A.D., the tradition of 'blooding' began.

Whenever a deer was killed, three drops of its blood was transferred by the tip of a knife and smeared on to the hunter's face — one on each cheek, the other on the forehead; the idea being to symbolise the cross or crucifix that Hubert reputedly saw between the antlers of that first deer.

What the Papers Say

August 12th is, of course, the start of the grouse shooting season and every year many of the papers make the usual gaffes about 'The Glorious Twelfth' – including the almost obligatory 'the crack of rifle fire over the moor'. Why they persist in this erroneous reporting every single year I've no idea, but they do.

Some will also make much of the cost of a shot grouse to the Gun and moor owner, and also may possible mention the tradition of birds being rushed down to London by helicopter so that the first of this year's birds can be enjoyed by the wealthy in the capital's top restaurants on the evening of the day they were shot. Undoubtedly, being the first to serve grouse is something of a tradition and, in the days before helicopters, it wasn't unknown for a moor owner to have his keeper shoot a couple of brace or so before the 12th and then have them motored down in order they were there ready and waiting for dinner on the opening day!

NOTHING TO GROUSE ABOUT

In an article published on the eve of the 2016 grouse shooting season, the *Daily Telegraph* carried – for the benefit of 'all you urbanites' – a list of facts about grouse compiled by Emily Allen. These included: 'Grouse are incredibly speedy ... [and] can fly at speeds of up to 70 miles per hour ... and have a habit of changing direction at the last minute.'

The piece also stressed the importance of heather in the daily diet of grouse and explained that: 'As well as berries and seeds, a typical grouse eats up to 50g of heather a day. They eat the young, tender heather with green shoots but nest and shelter in the old heather.' Somewhat frightening statistics pointed out that correctly maintained heather moorland is now rarer than rainforest (according to the Moorland Association) and that Britain 'has 75 per cent of what is left worldwide'. In addition, the writer mentioned the fact that 'red grouse are unique to Britain', and that the 'red grouse's closest relative, the willow grouse, is found throughout northern Europe, Asia, Canada and Alaska'.

Finally – and perfect for a book of this nature; dealing as it does, with facts, superstition and general quirkiness, the origin of the expression 'to grouse', meaning 'to complain or grumble', dates from the late nineteenth century, having apparently began life as soldiers' slang in the British Army ... and the earliest known use of the verb was made by Rudyard Kipling in 1887.

Government by paper

A. G. Street, my all-time favourite country writer, had this to say in a newspaper article he penned way back in 1935:

I have long felt that many of our national troubles are due to the fact that our administrators and their advisors live their lives too far away from the people to whom their decisions mean so much.

With that sentiment, I very much have to agree – some eighty plus years later, nothing much has changed.

IT'S IN THE PAPER — IT MUST BE TRUE!

Not infrequently during the season does the media attempt to run a story condemning game shooting. Quite often, the copy centres around the 'fact' that birds are reared and released to be shot for sport and then 'their bodies are dumped'.

One such article written by Colin Fernandez, environment correspondent for *The Daily Mail*, appeared in February 2016. The headline proclaimed that 'Some 30 pheasants were dumped after a shoot at a country estate' and that 'campaigners have branded it as "target practice with living creatures"'. Another [campaigner] asked to comment on the story said that 'it was unlikely that anyone was coming back to collect the birds'.

The article went on: 'Ed Shephard of the League Against Cruel Sports, who took undercover pictures across Britain during the shooting season which ended on February 1, said, "As the shooting party left, our investigators found these birds dumped on the side of the road just before it got dark."'

Fact or fancy? Myth or misinformation? With such reporting, how can the general public ever be expected to learn the truth that, considering the photograph that illustrated the article quite clearly showed freshly shot birds laid out to cool and tied together in braces, it was more likely to have been that the birds were left there for easy collection by the game cart between drives.

FINGERS CROSSED

As much of this book concerns facts, fallacies, myths and superstitions surrounding shooting and the countryside, I thought it appropriate to make mention of a survey that was reported by *MailOnline*.

Apparently, 'touching wood' is Britain's most popular superstitious belief and women are generally more superstitious than men … and the Scottish appeared to be the most superstitious people in the UK. Somewhat surprisingly, young people are more superstitious than older generations, therefore, it can only be assumed that a greater knowledge of science and technology has done nothing to stop people holding unusual beliefs.

In times of turbulent economic and political situations (when is it not?), people feel more superstitious and 'tend to worry about life, have a strong need for control, and feel uncomfortable with ambiguity'. As to actual figures, a total of 2,068 people took part in the survey and the results indicated that some 77 per cent were at least a little superstitious and/or engaged in some form of superstitious behaviour. So perhaps the rituals carried out by some Guns as outlined earlier ('SERIOUSLY SUPERSTITIOUS') begin to make a bit more sense now!

EARS AND HEADS

A magazine article in the shooting press touched on the subject of poaching – and pointed out that it was not the romantic rural pastime of an old country character taking a pheasant or rabbit for the pot. In fact, some modern poachers are not at all interested in putting meat on the table and illegal hare-coursing, for instance, is more about betting on the individual dog's ability to course.

The article also mentioned that another activity carried out by poachers 'involves placing bets on who can return to an agreed meeting point with the most deer ears' and further commented: 'It doesn't matter how the deer dies.' Along similar lines, pheasant release pens have been targeted: 'It's the pheasants' heads that they're after … Apparently, it's the lowlife who returns with the most heads that scoops the prize.'

HEADLINE NEWS

In *The Imperfect Shot* (Quiller, 2015), I mentioned the fact that newspapers tend to be a little flippant with the actual facts; especially when it comes to the topic of game shooting. Depending on their likely readership, copy editors tend to take a particular view — and provide somewhat overdramatic headlines such as these:

'Queen clubs bird to death': *Daily Mail* — after Her Majesty was seen dispatching a wounded pheasant brought to her by one of her dogs.

'Welby the one-shot wonder': *Sunday Times* — questioning current discussion at the time that Archbishop Justin Welby might have refused to be patron of the RSPCA because he once went on a pheasant shoot in the mid-1980s.

'Madonna bans shooting over fears of "hauntings" by dead animals': *Mail on Sunday* — reporting on the news that the singer had decided to ban shooting on the Wiltshire estate she owned at the time.

Damned with faint praise

Magazine and newspaper reviews can be quite damning – as evidenced by these comments from a somewhat cynical reviewer for *The Spectator* who, in September 1903, when charged with writing about the two volumes entitled *Shooting* (which appeared in *The Country Life Library of Sport* series), had this to say:

The two volumes contain a great number of photographs, some of which are excellent, whilst others will appeal to those who have never seen beaters crossing a bridge, or shooters about to sit down to their luncheon.

The present volume deals with shooting in its most modern aspect; it includes even a chapter by Mr Scott-Montagu on motor-cars for shooting purposes, which does not contain much new or useful information beyond the facts that motors go faster and further than horses, and do not catch cold or require to be fed or watched. He also points out that one can leave home a quarter of an hour later, and yet be back for a cup of tea before six. This chapter will appeal to every sportsman.

'Tweeded Toffs to Blast Grouse out of the Sky': *Morning Star* – at the start of the grouse shooting season.

'Beware invasion of the 50,000,000 pheasants as shooting season starts': *The Sunday Express* – before reporting that 'a record number of game birds will be released into the countryside as the shooting season begins this week'.

'"Is Pheasant Shooting Dangerous?" asks a weekly paper headline. We understand that many pheasants are of the opinion that it has its risks': *Punch* magazine 1917

RAPID RABBIT RETREAT!

Now here's a useful nugget to drop into the shoot lunch conversation! Apparently Napoleon's possibly most humiliating defeat wasn't that which resulted in his trudge through snow (and in Tchaikovsky composing the *1812 Overture*), but as a result of an encounter with rabbits!

In 1807, the 'Little Corporal' was in buoyant mood having signed the Peace of Tilsit, a landmark treaty between France, Russia and Prussia. And, in order to celebrate, he suggested that the imperial court should enjoy an afternoon's rabbit shooting.

The party arrived, the shoot commenced, and the gamekeepers went to drive the rabbits from the warrens. However, being more tame than wild, they thought they were going to be fed and, mistaking Napoleon for the warrener who normally brought them their food, headed at great speed towards him. Somewhat disconcerted, according to contemporary newspaper accounts of the fiasco; '... the emperor of France sped off in his coach, comprehensively beaten and covered in shame ...'

Mistaking Napoleon for the warrener

MAKING CONTACT

In modern times, rather than reading a newspaper, there's many who keep in touch with the world via smartphone ... and there's many a tale of shooting people who, on getting their smartphone out at the meeting point or at the first drive, are berated by their fellow sportsmen and women.

Some stories are no doubt exaggerated (we all know of mobile phones being stamped upon or thrown into the nearest piece of water by irate hosts!) but, for some, despite being out in the countryside, it's apparently important to get an occasional fix of city life by going on Twitter or checking your emails. Toby Young, associate editor of *The Spectator*, once described how difficult getting an internet connection may be:

> ... quite apart from poor network coverage and the scarcity of Wi-Fi — far rarer than the lesser-spotted cormorant — it appears to be against the law to connect to the internet in the country. I don't mean you'll be arrested, which is unlikely because rural England is almost entirely unpoliced. I mean that if you get out your iPhone in public, you immediately attract gamma-rays of hostility from everyone in the immediate vicinity.

No 'talk-talk' on Virgin mobiles

Up until a couple of seasons ago, game shooting enthusiasts using Virgin mobile phones were unable to visit shooting websites as, in their infinite wisdom, Virgin had installed complex under-18 filters as default settings on their mobile phone network – which meant that any websites connected to

shooting issues were inaccessible to users. However, after some extensive talks and lobbying from the BASC, the issue was eventually resolved.

As a spokesman for Virgin Media told *The Shooting Times* back in 2013: 'In line with the agreed industry approach, we restrict mobile access to content suitable for over-18s only. As soon as the British Association for Shooting and Conservation got in touch, we looked into the matter and are working with our network partner to ensure [that shooting websites are] removed from our content filter.'

QUACKERS!

In June 2015, *The Huffington Post* carried a story regarding the fact that the Canal and River Trust, which preserves more than 2,000 miles of waterways throughout England and Wales, had created lanes exclusively for waterfowl on towpaths and similar areas in London, Birmingham and Manchester. To this end, white lines demarcating areas only to be used by the wildfowl had been painted and, so that the birds in question couldn't possibly get things wrong, a stencilled silhouette of a duck was added.

AND FINALLY ...!

In a fairly balanced report on grouse shooting published on 12 August 2015, Stephanie Linning, for *MailOnline*, put both sides of the argument regarding the ethics of grouse shooting, economics and moorland management — and concluded by saying:

> But the League Against Cruel Sports is urging restaurants not to serve grouse because of the 'by-catch' of other wild animals it causes, caught in snares used to protect birds from predators, the shooting and snaring

of mountain hares in the Scottish Highlands over disease concerns, and birds of prey illegally persecuted.

A previous director of campaigns for the organisation said: 'The collateral damage caused by getting a grouse to the table leaves a nasty taste in the mouth.' He said people were giving the impression shooting game for the table was healthy, sustainable and environmentally friendly, but that it was none of those things. 'Millions of other animals and birds are deliberately killed to protect the grouse shooting industry,' he said. 'The environment is being devastated by the burning of grouse moors, and millions of tonnes of lead shot are left to poison the countryside.

As can be seen when the topic of lead shot is mentioned elsewhere in this book, the facts appear to indicate otherwise.

Choose Your
Weapons

Guns (and to some extent) knives, obviously need to be treated with respect – and, when it comes to the legalities, use, keeping and handling of guns, there is no room for complacency. There are, though, several myths and misconceptions bandied about amongst the shooting fraternity and it's essential that one is familiar with the facts before getting out on to the shooting field.

It is similar with knives – particularly when it comes to the length of blade one is allowed to carry legally. Of course, it all depends on what it is you're doing – a big-bladed knife is a practical item of equipment for the deer stalker but is, arguably, not needed attached to one's belt Crocodile Dundee style, on a partridge day. We all need a penknife though: they have a multitude of uses ranging from slicing open a 'slab' of cartridges to cutting a piece of baler twine to use as a makeshift dog lead.

LEAD SHOT ... OR NOT?

For several years it's been illegal to use cartridges containing lead shot on the foreshore and around Sites of Special Scientific Interest (SSSI). The BASC's website (*www.basc.org.uk/lead*) has this to say:

It's just not 'done'!

The laws and legalities of using knives and guns are complicated enough – but so too are those pertaining to wildfowling from a boat. In most instances only non-motorised watercraft such as punts or rowing boats are allowed – although, should you ever find yourself duck-shooting in America, you can, apparently, use a motor boat operating at a speed of 5 knots or less in order to retrieve dead or wounded ducks.

So, whilst in certain countries, 'aircraft, motor boats or motor vehicles must not be used to pursue, hunt, take or destroy game', in France, similar legislation also includes the fact that it's illegal to shoot game from a bicycle ... even if wearing stereotypical beret, striped T-shirt and a garland of onions!

In England the lead shot regulations ban the use of lead shot over all foreshore, over specified SSSIs, and for the shooting of all ducks and geese, coot and moorhen – wherever they occur. The Welsh Assembly introduced similar regulations in September 2002.

Scotland's regulations came into force at the end of March 2005 and Northern Ireland came into force in September 2009.

In Northern Ireland the lead shot regulations are based on the Scottish approach and prohibit the use of lead shot on or over any area of wetland for any shooting activity.

Wetlands are defined as, regardless of size, any areas of foreshore, marsh, fen, peatland with standing water, regularly or seasonally flooded fields, and other water sources whether they be natural or man-made, static or flowing, fresh, brackish or salt.

IT'S AN AGE THING

Myth and misinformation abounds when it comes to young Guns and the laws concerning shotgun certificates. It's a complicated matter but generally, the following applies:

- Someone under the age of fifteen may possess a shotgun only if supervised by a person aged twenty-one or over; or if the gun is in a gun cover and therefore cannot be readily fired. In addition, it is an offence for a young person under fifteen to buy or hire a shotgun (and/or cartridges). Also — and it's well worth any good intentioned parent taking note — it is an offence to gift a shotgun to anyone under the age of fifteen.

- Despite the above stipulations, it is, however, possible for a person under fifteen to hold their own shotgun certificate — but can only use (not own) a gun whilst under the supervision of someone aged twenty-one or over. The period of 'loan' of such a gun can only be for a maximum of seventy-two hours — and the gun can only be used on private land.

- Anyone aged between fifteen and seventeen who is the holder of a shotgun certificate may be lent or given a gun and cartridges by another certificate holder for up to seventy-two hours — and can use the gun on private land without supervision.

- Those aged eighteen (or over) — and who are holders of shotgun certificates — may buy or hire a shotgun and ammunition suitable for that gun.

Choose your weapons

FIRE ROUND CORNERS

Most of us probably think that the better gun stocks have always been made of walnut. As an excellent article in the March 2016 issue of *The Field* had it: 'It is light, strong, easily worked and … if you carve a little cast into it, it won't get bent out of shape.'

Stocks have, however, over the years, been made from material as diverse as elephant ivory, rhino horn and, on the wood front, Bird's-eye maple, birch and beech. The cheaper, more accessible woods are, as one might reasonably assume, more generally found on some of the cheaper weapons such as Baikal; guns that, as many a keeper who uses one in their day-to-day work (rather than risking their 'best') will tell you, 'can fire round corners and what it doesn't kill, will bring back prisoner.' Some even maintain that such a gun is robust enough to hammer in an errant fence post but that is, I think, taking their gun's usefulness just that little too far!

WAXING LYRICAL

In answer to the question: 'What should I use to clean my walnut stock before applying wax?' when it appeared on an American website in September 2015, respondent 'DanielM' had this comment to make:

> It depends on what finish it has, and what you want to clean from it. Mostly it would just be a wipe down with a clean cloth to remove any dust, dirt, or blood (best to do the last while it is fresh, as it sets like enamel if you don't — don't ask how I know. Blood also promotes rust if you get it on the metalwork). That should really be it.
>
> If it has stains around the action from where gun oil has soaked in, you can often reduce these by putting a bit of talcum powder or powdered chalk on them, and leaving the stock in the sun. The oil rises

and is absorbed into the powder. You can clean out checkering with a stiff brush and some turpentine. For an oil-finished stock that has too much oil buildup on the surface a bit of turps on a rag will take it back too.

PULL THROUGH AND WIPE DOWN!

There are lots of tradition and 'tricks of the trade' associated with cleaning your shotgun after use. Sadly, few of us have a servant on hand to do it for us — unlike at the beginning of the last century when, as W. Greener noted in his book, *The Gun and its Development*: 'If a gun be wet, it should be wiped dry at once, but the cleaning of the barrels and breech-action may be left until the sportsman or his servant has time to do it properly.'

Greener then went on to describe the use of oil, turpentine, refined neatsfoot, pure Arctic sperm oil, Vaseline, linseed oil, chronometer oil, Rangoon oil and Russian tallow, but warned his readers to avoid emery cloth for removing leading, or a feather 'for the purpose of putting on any lubricant'.

Rust-busters

A recent online forum discussion talked of various tips and wrinkles used by modern day shotgun users. The use of 0000 grade wire wool was recommended by one to remove rust spots, while another thought 'Autosol' or 'T-cut' the perfect solution. To protect the barrels from moisture, it was suggested that 'acf50', an anti-corrosion formula used to protect aircraft from corrosion on aircraft carriers, would do the job — a sledgehammer to crack a nut maybe!

When the gun is in the cabinet (some favour having the barrels pointing downwards), a VP90 corrosion inhibitor sachet stuck inside the cabinet door is 'supposed to last a year and coat everything in a vapour to stop air contact'. Otherwise, several of the small sachets of silicone gel will apparently act in a similar fashion.

TWO OF A KIND

Although not many of us are lucky to own them, everyone knows that two guns made at the same time by the same gunmaker, marked with consecutive serial numbers underneath and '1' and '2' on the top, are a 'pair'. Three such guns are, logically enough, a 'trio' but somewhat bizarrely, four identical shotguns are known by most in the trade as being a 'set of four' rather than as a 'quadruple' or similar.

Two of a kind

PROOF OF THE PUDDING

Periodically some celebrity is shown in the media as having been given the freedom of the city and thus becoming a 'freeman' of say, the City of London. Steeped in tradition and accompanied by dark tales of strange handshakes and odd rituals, it's actually all to do with the various livery companies — one of which is the Worshipful Company of Gunmakers, which was granted a Royal Charter in 1637.

Its aim was (and is) to regulate the gun-making trade; a vital part of which appertains to the safety of a gun and its suitability to be stamped with legally required proof marks. As the Worshipful Company's website (*www.gunmakers. norg.uk*) points out, although more modern inspection techniques are also used: 'It is still done as it has been since the Company was established in 1637: by firing the gun with an over-pressure charge of powder ...'

The Gun Barrel Proof Acts (*www.legislation.gov.uk/ukpga/1978/9*) dictate the actual specification and 'require proof for all guns sold in the United Kingdom, and for guns that have undergone structural modifications to pressure-bearing parts ...', as well as for those imported from other countries. More than three-and-a-half centuries on, the British proof mark remains the same: a stamp of the letters 'GP' surmounted by a crown. Only the Company can bestow it, and it is illegal to sell a gun without it.

Elsewhere, several of the Worshipful Companies have connections with field sports, no matter how tenuous. Andrew Johnston, managing director of Quiller, mentions that he has a stag's head hanging on the wall 'from the beast that my grandfather shot in 1934 when he was the Master Cutler in Sheffield and it was the tradition that the Master Cutler provided the venison for the annual dinner'.

NB: There are still around 125 City of London Livery Companies in existence today — to see if there's one relevant to your trade or craft, visit: *www. cityoflondon.gov.uk/about-the-city*

THE KNIVES ARE OUT

Talk of the Master Cutlers of Sheffield (*see above*) is as good a reason as any to mention the fact that Sheffield was, in its Victorian heyday, the centre for not just domestic cutlery, but also the making of pocket-knives, many of which were exported in vast quantities to the US and the colonies. The 'Barlow' knife was originally of British manufacture and was one particularly favoured by the hobos of America during the late nineteenth century – as evidenced by Mark Twain, writing in *The Adventures of Huckleberry Finn*:

> All the stores was along one street. They had white domestic awnings in front, and the country-people hitched their horses to the awning-posts. There was empty dry-goods boxes under the awnings, and loafers roosting on them all day long, whittling them with their Barlow knives; and chawing tobacco, and gaping and yawning and stretching – a mighty ornery lot.

At one time in the UK, virtually every child and country-living person would have had a penknife in their pocket. Nowadays, to be found with such a 'weapon' about their person for no real reason leaves its owner open to the accusation of having suspicious motives. Hopefully, though, it will be a long time before Gun, stalker, gamekeeper, picker-up or fisherman will have to relinquish possession of a knife suited (and essential) to their work and sport.

Knives are always a good present to give – but one should, however, remember that it's bad luck to actually 'gift' a knife. Tradition has it that payment must always be made. Therefore, as the giver, always insist on at least a 2p piece in return and, as the recipient, straight away dig into your pocket for a coin to offer back.

On the cutting edge

Other superstitions connected with knife-ownership include:

- In Finland, a knife given as a gift is a sign of respect. This is especially true for various clubs and organizations, privately or government held. The knife, a Finnish fixed blade outdoor knife called a 'Puukko', is given to trusted employers or contacts and always presented with the handle first to signify trust and friendly intentions.

- Placing a knife under the bed of a woman giving birth is believed to ease her pain during labour.

- Sticking a knife into a cradle's headboard is thought to protect the baby.

- Two knives crossed on a table will cause a quarrel. It is believed that uncrossing or straightening them immediately will prevent bad luck or a quarrel from happening.

- Never stir anything using your knife (such as soup or coffee) because that brings bad luck — and also the possibility of a bad stomach if you've just been using the knife for paunching rabbits or gralloching deer!

- Some knife owners believe that you should never close a knife (either folding it in or putting it back in its sheath) if someone else has opened it because it is bad luck. Some have apparently even given knives away just because this happened.

- You can never be said to truly own a knife unless it has 'bitten' you (tasted your blood). A similar superstition states that a knife that has 'bitten' its owner will stay sharp longer.

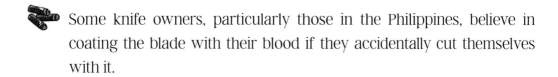

Some knife owners, particularly those in the Philippines, believe in coating the blade with their blood if they accidentally cut themselves with it.

Bad things will happen if a knife falls and sticks, point-end, into the floor.

A knife made of steel is believed to protect you against curses and fairies.

THE ROAD TO DAMASCUS

In the hugely successful *Game of Thrones* books and subsequent television series, the blades of some of the characters' weapons are forged from a super-strong, but incredibly light substance known as Valyrian steel. Although created in the imagination of author George R. Martin, he based Valyrian steel on a real-life alloy referred to as Damascus steel — which is well-known as the metal used on some knives and, of course, in the manufacture of gun barrels.

Developed in India and the Middle East, Damascus steel was known for its super-strong, super-sharp qualities, and for its distinctive rippled surface, but it took European conquests in the east during the 1500s to bring the idea of spiral-welded gun barrels to the attention of a wider clientele.

Originally knives and weapons were made from what was known as 'Wootz' steel and came from a specific ore mine in India. To find a gun made from such steel would be rare, if not impossible, and even as long ago as 1858, William Greener noted that, instead of using wootz steel, the more common option was to use pattern welded steel — and the reason that they were called Damascus barrels was because the patterns on the welded steel resembled that of the original metal. Basically then, pattern-welded 'Damascus' steel was (and is) made by arranging pieces of iron and steel, or two or more different types of steel together, to create specific patterns in the finished product.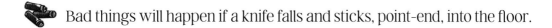

Gamekeepers and Gamekeeping

GROUSE

Sometimes it is necessary for the shooting person (and other country sports enthusiasts) to justify their sport — and it helps if you have the facts and arguments to hand. As we've already seen in an earlier chapter, in the press and social media there's a vast amount of erroneous and negative information offered by the so-called conservation experts who wish to see shooting and other country sports banned — and keepers often bear the brunt of it. It was then, a pleasure to read naturalist, birder, writer and conservation scientist, James Common's conclusion to his online article, *A Summer on a Scottish Grouse Moor*:

> I spent the summer on a grouse moor and thoroughly enjoyed it … In addition to the great wildlife I also very much enjoyed getting to know the team of gamekeepers working on the estate. Yes these people shoot

and trap legal quarry, yes they carry guns but many also boast an uncanny knowledge of local wildlife and all were more than happy to facilitate my viewing on the site's wildlife. On top of this they also worked incessantly, day and night, in all weather conditions, I certainly could not do it. I now no longer think of gamekeepers as the 'enemy'...

The curmudgeonly keeper!

Richard Jefferies, although ready to sing the praises of the Victorian keeper, wasn't afraid to mention the other side of his character – as he did in the classic, *The Gamekeeper at Home*:

He has his faults: notably, a hastiness of temper towards his undermen, and towards labourers who transgress his rules. He is apt to use his ground-ash stick rather freely without thought of consequences ... When he takes a dislike or suspicion of a man, nothing will move it; he is stubbornly inimical and unforgiving, totally incapable of comprehending the idea of loving an enemy.

A PRICE ON THEIR HEADS

Some in the media would have it that modern day gamekeepers are doing nothing for the welfare of wildlife. However, history says that it was the Tudors who drove wildlife close to extinction due to bounty hunting brought about by Henry VIII.

Apparently, during his reign, 'millions of birds and animals were slaughtered' in England and Wales as a result of The Preservation of Grain Act, passed in 1532 by Henry VIII and strengthened by Elizabeth I in 1566. The Act made it compulsory for every man, woman and child to kill as many creatures as possible that appeared on an official list of 'vermin'.

In 2010, Roger Lovegrove, former director of the Royal Society for the Protection of Birds (RSPB), published the findings of six years' research in his book, *Silent Fields: The Long Decline of a Nation's Wildlife*. In it he claimed that, 'the impact has been catastrophic,' and: 'Until now, we believed that many creatures currently facing extinction owed their fate to nineteenth century gamekeepers and environmental changes,' he said.

Henry VIII's Act was drawn up to counter food shortages and spread of disease caused by a series of bad harvests and a sharp rise in population. The king himself imposed a bounty on each creature, ranging from a penny for the head of a kite or a raven to 12 pence for a badger or a fox — which were considerable sums when the average agricultural wage was around four pence a day.

All parishes had to raise a levy to pay for the bounties, while communities that failed to kill enough animals were punished with fines. 'The inducements appeared to be successful,' noted Lovegrove, who studied medieval archives from more than 15,000 parishes in England and Wales that recorded the slaughter of millions of birds and mammals between the mid-sixteenth and mid-eighteenth centuries. 'I uncovered evidence in the parish records of a frenzy of killing that continued for many decades.'

Undoubtedly, today's far more enlightened countryside management and conservation programmes are the far better option!

REARING — THEN AND NOW

Victorian keepers would, with the aid of broody hens, carefully concocted foods and twenty-four-hour personal protection, rear pheasants from eggs to the age of six weeks before carefully releasing them into suitable woodland. Their rearing field was a hive of activity: rows and rows of broody boxes led on to line upon line of small coops, into which the broody hen and her chicks were placed after hatching. The hen was incarcerated but the chicks could (after a couple of days of being kept close to Mum by the judicious placing of two boards to form a triangle to the coop front), run freely and would come rushing back to their coop whenever the mother hen called. At some vantage point would be positioned the keeper's hut, in which regular food mixtures were created from freshly cooked rabbit meat, fresh greens and ground cereals.

Scientifically formulated compound crumbs and pellets have usurped the secret recipes cooked and manufactured on a daily basis and modern incubators and brooding equipment have done away with the need for a single broody hen. Gone are the coops that used to be taken to a carefully chosen woodland ride – complete with hen and poults – on the back of a horse-drawn flatbed trailer and in their place are large, specially constructed release pens. It is, however, important to remember that today's rearing and releasing principles were first put into practice by the Victorian gamekeeper.

Put a sock on it

In the days when broody hens were the only option, each hen and her chicks would be placed in a coop with bars running vertically along the front through which the pheasant or partridge chicks could run freely, but the broody hen could not. She could, however put her head and neck through for food and water and, if her chicks wandered too far, or an avian predator flew over, she would call them back to the safety of the coop.

Sometimes the coop was fitted with a low run for extra security but, in the days when hatching and rearing with broody hens first began, most keepers used only a coop. As dusk fell, it was necessary to shut the chicks in with their foster mother for the night – not always an easy task. To make their approach to the coop as quiet as possible, keepers would often put socks over their boots for when they crept up to it – the slightest noise would scare the chicks and they would run out ... and the keeper would then have to wait until they had settled again.

GAMEKEEPING EXTRA CURRICULAR

Whilst today's keepers are totally au fait with modern practice necessary for success, if you can believe what you read, being a gamekeeper also brings with it a certain earthy and lusty status when it comes to success with the ladies! Was there ever a real-life scenario such as portrayed by D. H. Lawrence in his infamous book, *Lady Chatterley's Lover?* According to David S. D. Jones, writing in *Gamekeeping: An Illustrated History* (2014), whilst this kind of liaison was not common, it was not unknown — and that despite the fact that, as Jones notes: 'Any keeper who was caught fraternizing with the wife or daughter of his employer would be instantly dismissed without a reference,' making it impossible to find a job on another estate.

However, when the boot was on the other foot, so to speak, it was relatively common for a landowner to have a secret affair with a servant girl that, as is the way with such things, occasionally resulted in the birth of a child. As Jones further comments: 'Many of these "natural children" were brought up by families on the estate, where they later often became gamekeepers, or gamekeepers' wives.'

That's no lady!

As to whether there was ever a real-life Lady Chatterley, some think there was and that Lawrence's character of Constance was based on Lady Ottoline Morrell, wife of Liberal MP Philip Morrell.

A part of the Bloomsbury 'set' (famous for 'living in squares and loving in triangles'!), Lady Ottoline (1873–1938) was, according to academic professor, Hermione Lee, 'legendarily idiosyncratic … Her amazing looks were at once sexy and grotesque. She was very tall, with a huge head of copper-coloured hair, turquoise eyes and great beaky features. She wore fantastical highly coloured clothes and hats with great style and bravado.'

A first cousin of Elizabeth Bowes Lyon — the future Queen Mother — she was extremely well connected yet, despite that (or perhaps because of it), her affairs were well-known. Whilst no one has ever suggested that Lawrence at any time succumbed to her undoubted charms, he was, nonetheless, a frequent visitor to both her London home and her country house near Oxford.

As to the identity of Lady Morrell's possible working class lover — and the inspiration for the character of Mellors — it rather spoils the story to have to say that it is thought he was a stonemason who installed some garden statues, rather than a gamekeeper on the Morrell's Oxfordshire estate.

GAME GIRLS

Female gamekeepers were almost unheard of when *Lady Chatterley's Lover* shocked the world all those years ago. Almost unheard of, but not totally ; in the Victorian era there lived the redoubtable Mary (sometimes known as 'Polly') Fishburne who was, for several years, employed as keeper by the Earl of Leicester at Holkham Hall, Norfolk. Described by one employer as having, 'large black eyes, red cheeks, and white teeth, her hair was cropped like a man's, and she wore a man's hat. The rest of her attire was feminine. She was irreproachable in conduct ...' Further accounts after her death in 1873 report that: 'Neither her fine looks of manly womanhood nor her anecdotes of Holkham and her own former powers with dogs and guns will soon be forgotten by those who knew her.'

Whilst there are, nowadays, syndicates of lady Guns; teams of lady loaders and pickers-up, why are there not more lady keepers in the twenty-first century? It was the likes of Jill Mason who, in the late 1960s world of Germaine Greer, equal rights and bra-burning, led what might easily have become a flood of females into the male-dominated keepering profession – but which, as it turns out, has never ever been much more than a trickle. Mason, one of England's first professional lady keepers and nowadays even more well-known as a country writer and author, recollects:

I suppose I was a bit of a pioneer in that field. It wasn't something I particularly planned on doing – I just dropped into it when David [her husband] had taken a single-handed position and, in the middle of his first rearing season, damaged his knee. That was back in 1969.

Nowadays that would be fixed with micro-surgery, but then it meant being in hospital for two weeks with six weeks' recuperation afterwards. When I left school I'd worked on a poultry rearing farm so taking over caring for the incubators and rearing chicks was no big deal.

Working with him progressed from there and was to last for thirty years ...

A college lecturer recently mentioned that, in his experience, 'female gamekeeping students are almost always better than males when it comes to rearing ... they have a far greater attention to detail and, when it comes to the subject of gamekeeping being hard physical work, girls will always find a way of getting round the problem.'

Mason further opines that women 'are very likely to be more conscientious than men in all aspects ... and more patient. Apart from this being in most women's nature, there is also the feeling that, working in a man's world, they have a point to prove. However, the downside is the lack of physical strength ... but I suppose modern keepering has changed so much it is no longer such an issue.'

Keepering has undoubtedly changed in recent years and, in many cases, technology has come to the rescue. So then, for either male or female, all that is required is dedication to the job, general fitness and overall good health.

DOGGING — OR DOGGING-IN?

It's as well to know some of the correct terminology when it comes to gamekeeping talk — a gamekeeper might well give a totally different answer to the question 'do you go dogging?' as opposed to 'do you go dogging-in? It's only a subtle difference but it's a very important one!

As Peter Holt explained in his book *The Keen Countryman's Miscellany* (2012): 'One of the more earthy country sports to gain popularity in twenty-first century Britain is the sexual practice of dogging, which involves couples having it off with strangers in cars in front of strangers in remote rural locations.' Dogging-in, on the other hand, is simply the practice of using gun dogs to push wandering pheasants homewards from the shoot boundaries!

There are lots of archaic terms and names when it comes shooting and country sports — so much so that the rather appropriately named C. E. Hare wrote a book about them way back in 1939. In *The Language of Field Sports*, he tells us that a group of pheasants are referred to as a 'nye' whilst a young family of the same is a 'brood' or 'bouquet'; a group of ducks on the water are known as a 'paddling' whilst in flight they are referred to as a 'team', and that group terms for wildfowl in general include a 'trip' or a 'plump' but specific terms for widgeon include a 'flight' ... or, when they are on the water, a 'bunch', 'company' or 'knob'. Whilst out and about, you might see a 'tiding' of magpies and a 'murder' of crows; a 'host' of sparrows or a 'team', 'bank', 'wedge', 'herd' or 'bevy' of swans.

More recently, one of *The Field* magazine's columnists reminded readers that, 'we call "Mark cock" when we see woodcock, but "Cock forrard" for a cock pheasant'. One should then, perhaps be particularly careful when stringing together a sentence that mentions both 'dogging-in' and the fact that a male pheasant has risen!

Just saying

There are several sayings appertaining to shooting and keeping. Take, for instance, the fact that it's easy to tell the difference between a stoat and a weasel because:
'A weasel is weasely distinguished as a stoat is stoatally different!'

Also: 'If you see one rook, it's a crow but if you see lots of crows, they're rooks,' (referring to the generalisation that rooks tend to congregate in flocks whereas crows are more usually seen either alone or as a pair). Another well-known saying is the one that tells you: 'If a crouching hare remains the same size as you walk up to it, it's a stone – but if a stone gets smaller on your approach; it was a hare'!

PHEASANTS AND FOXES

Now here's an interesting thing. Way back when (and there's no publishing date – only the fact that it was published by the Cotswold Game Farm and cost three shillings and sixpence) the booklet, *Shoot Management*, written by P. R. Symonds, stated that:

There are few better ways of teaching young pheasant their way around than by letting hounds draw the covert. This has the dual advantage of making both pheasant and fox afraid of man and dog. A tame pheasant will never give good sport. An unhunted fox soon becomes much too bold and can then cause a lot of damage ... To avoid accidents the master of the local pack should be advised of shooting dates as early as possible.

Symonds' statement shows how things have changed in the gamekeeping and hunting world. At one time it was a regular thing for shooting estates to host the hounds and, as mentioned, it was considered a 'good thing', particularly early in the season, as a means to get young birds to fly well. The first visits would, depending on harvest, occur during early September cub-hunting mornings.

Ever since the Hunting Act 2004, cub-hunting has become more correctly known as hound training and, rather than dispersing litters of young cubs as was the original intent, it's purpose is, as the name suggests, to educate young hounds and enter them into trail-hunting.

Love-hate relationship

Keepers and huntsmen have long had a 'love-hate' relationship — at least according to countryside myth and rural gossip. The truth is, however, somewhat different and, especially in this day and age when field sports in general are coming under attack from those who, despite having no knowledge on the subject, wish to see them banned, it's important that shooting and hunting co-exist happily together.

The internal conflict between keepers and hunting probably began in the days where the keeper's boss was also the Master of Hounds (a common enough situation) and was expected to 'keep' a fox for the days when hounds met on the estate. The prospect of a pack of hounds running riot through the keeper's carefully tended pheasant coverts didn't much appeal either but, in actual fact, research done back in the late 1960s and 1970s seemed to prove that, if hounds were hard on a scent rather than actually drawing for a fox, hounds could visit one day and a perfect pheasant shoot be enjoyed the next.

'Not the done thing, old boy!'

There are stories of keepers (and even Guns) shooting a hunted fox in front of hounds — one account of such an instance, written between the two world wars, comes from an unnamed master:

> During a fast hunt … I heard a shot fired in front of hounds and galloping round some bushes was confronted by an excited sportsman, holding in one hand a smoking gun and in the other, his hat. He rushed up shouting that he'd 'missed the fox but that he's only a short way ahead and your dogs may yet catch him.'

Big Bags,
Roadkill and
Bragging Rights

'It's not about the bag, it's more about the day out' – or so say so many of those who enjoy a day's shooting. And so it is; however, I venture to suggest that a driven day that sees a paucity of grouse, pheasants or partridge will soon be commented on in the shoot room at lunchtime, or amongst travelling companions on the way home. There's a happy medium.

It's true that few want to emulate the big bags of yesteryear but, when all has gone well and one has been fortunate enough to be the keeper, the host or a guest on a day that has been perfect, it's difficult not to brag. Conversely, on a day when things have not come up to expectation and there's not enough in the bag for everyone to take a brace home, it may be necessary to resort to roadkill picked up en route in order to save face!

KEEP IT REAL

Generally speaking, any team that's achieving a three-to-one cartridge/kill ratio is probably about or slightly above average. When planning a day – and despite what the team of Guns may say – very few want extremely difficult, almost impossible to hit birds presented on the first drive and it's best to lead up to such things gently. Giving the Guns a slightly less challenging first drive often helps make the day go well, simply because it instils confidence.

Once they've 'got their eye' in, however, it's a totally different matter, and the correct mix of high drives and well-populated covers from which birds provide a good yet not overly difficult shot will all help to ensure that your guest Guns achieve their perfect bag for the day.

As to the best drives, most keepers will tell you that they aim (no pun intended) to give them as the last drive before lunch and as the last drive of the day ... the theory being that, as the Guns go in for lunch or go home for the day, they'll be left thinking that the whole morning/day has been a good one (and the Gun's 'tips' reflect that fact!)

BIG BAGS

The shooting world is full of supposed facts and figures when it comes to the subject of big bags and shooting day records. In the manner of fishermen's tales and 'the one that got away', these sometimes tend to get embroidered upon over the years but, nevertheless, there are some remarkable, verified accounts in existence. The names of Lord Ripon, Maharajah Duleep Singh and the Duke of Portland (who, towards the end of his life said: 'When I look back at the game book, I am quite ashamed of the enormous number of pheasants we sometimes killed.') are frequently mentioned whenever the subject is being discussed but other, less well-known 'sportsmen' achieved some incredible bags.

In October 1898, at Blenheim Palace, Oxfordshire, the Duke of Marlborough's shooting guests accounted for 6,943 rabbits, whilst in Hungary in December 1909, Count Karolyi and his cronies finished the day with a bag of some 6,125 pheasants.

Going it alone, Lord Walsingham famously shot 1,070 grouse to his own gun at Blubberhouses, Yorkshire, on 30 August 1888. In Ireland, in the season 1879–80, professional wildfowler Patrick Halloran killed, to his own gun, 2,000 snipe – and, during his lifetime, it's reckoned he shot well over 40,000. One day, in 1924 (his last season), he managed to bag nine snipe with six shots when three rose together and he killed them with one shot.

One hundred, not out

Pat Strutt was born in 1895 and died in 1999, aged 104. She shot her first stag on the family Kingairlock Estate in 1912 at the age of seventeen – and was still climbing and stalking totally unaided in the Kingairlock Hills when she was eighty-five years of age. During the intervening years, her game diaries showed that she had shot some 2,000 deer.

COUNTING THE BAG – EUROPEAN-STYLE

Should you ever be invited, it's as well to know that, in many European countries, especially those such as Bulgaria, Croatia and Slovenia, there is a tremendous amount of tradition attached to the end of the day: not only is the bag ceremonially counted in front of the Guns, but it is also laid out in a set formation.

Generally, whatever has been shot is laid out on its right-hand side and, as the bag is counted (almost always from left to right), every tenth bird is moved out slightly from the row. On a day when both birds and beasts are on the list, the game is laid out according to its weight, size and sex. Whoever is responsible for the counting must only go up and down the rows and never actually step over any of the carcasses whilst doing so. Symbolic bonfires may be lit at each corner of the patch of ground where the game is laid and hunting horns will almost certainly be blown.

On occasion, pine tree branches will be laid over the bodies or small sprigs placed in the mouths of game such as deer. With the latter, don't think that it's a simple case of just picking up and using any old fir branch: it must be snapped, not cut, from a location quite close to where the majority of the game has been shot and should be roughly the size of an outstretched hand.

Traditionally, the twig or branch is then split into three sections; the first being placed in the animal's mouth to represent its last meal, the second on the flank of the beast, and the third gently dipped in its blood before being inserted in the right-hand side of the hunter's hat band. Although perhaps less common nowadays, in times gone by, such branches would then be kept and saved in a box until New Year's Eve, when the sportsman would remove each one-by-one in order to reminisce and relive his season's hunting exploits.

TO HANG OR NOT TO HANG

There's a lot talked about hanging game once it's been shot. Large sporting estates have always had a game larder — architecturally, they were often ornate and quite splendid affairs. To conform to 2006 food hygiene regulations, you might need to store your game in a chilled unit prior to its collection by the game dealer (you might also need to have completed a game-handling course — for more information on which, see: *www.reading.ac.uk/foodlaw/pdf/uk-05048-wild-game-guidance.pdf*)

At the risk of teaching 'grandmother to suck eggs' and possibly insulting the intelligence of the more experienced, traditionally, game birds are hung by their heads whilst rabbits, hares and the carcasses of boar or venison are hung by their back legs, heads facing downwards.

Hares are unusual in that they are normally hung with their guts still in, whereas rabbits and deer have their intestines removed as soon as possible after being killed. Wild duck are not generally hung (but see Rose Henniker Heaton's observations below) as, for some reason, the practice does not seem to improve their flavour: however, if you have a particular yeaning to do so, they, unlike pheasants and partridge, are normally hung by their feet.

In 1931, in her book, *The Perfect Hostess*, Rose Henniker Heaton, suggested that:

It is not possible to lay down any hard and fast rules about the right moment to eat game. It depends entirely on the weather and the state of birds (if badly shot, or if old, or young). If a bird is old, it keeps longer, and is better for keeping so long as it is dry and not mauled in any way. Of course, late in the season the birds keep much longer. Woodcock, snipe and plover should be eaten fresh. The great thing is slow cooking and plenty of basting:

Grouse – keep a few days if weather permits.
Pheasant – hang four to five days if weather permits.
Partridge – keep a few days if weather permits.
Wild duck – keep a few days if possible.
Wild pigeon – eat fresh.

The arrival of oven-ready game, pre-packed and labelled is, to some, 'a mixed blessing' as it makes no allowance for individual taste with regard to hanging times. On the other hand, it is so very convenient and easily sourced!

IT'S ALL A MATTER OF TASTE!

As Carolyn Little, writing in her book, *The Game Cook* (Crowood Press, 1998), remarks: 'The days when game cookery was limited to the realms of the private country house party or the farmer's house and keeper's cottage are gone.'

It's long been accepted that game is good for you – with the reasons given being that it's low in fat and has lived a free-range sort of life ... and so it is and has. There are certainly no myths and fallacies about that!

Each year, in November, the Countryside Alliance and the British Association for Shooting and Conservation (BASC) combine their 'Game to Eat' and 'Taste of Game' campaigns in order to create 'Great British Game Week' and, every year, more and more restaurants and pubs cook up new and exciting dishes so as to introduce game to new audiences.

Even roadkill has its dedicated followers; the most notable of whom is someone who has the (enviable?) reputation of being considered the 'roadkill connoisseur of Cornwall'.

Presumably, however, not all of what he claims to have cooked and enjoyed has been found alongside a Cornish lane:

I have eaten rabbit, blue hare, brown hare, pheasant, partridge, fallow deer, roe deer, muntjac, badger, otter, fox, vole, horseshoe bat, long-eared bat, barn owl, porcupine, possum, gallinule, kea, wallaby, wood pigeon, racing pigeon, feral pigeon, collared dove, rook, swan, duck, moorhen, grouse, blackbird, Canada goose, cat, dog, stoat, grass snake, sheep, and possibly others.

Whilst some proclaim that roadkill is; 'lean, healthy, organic, free, guilt-free and as fresh as fresh can be', others – the Food Standards Agency, for example – suggest that, as food, it runs 'the risk of disease, contamination, and bacteria'. Generally, though, game as we more usually obtain it, is healthy, traceable and, within the jurisdiction of estate management, has been produced within reasonably strict welfare and food standard guidelines.

In the confessional

Country folk have long had a taste for what's available on their doorstep. In a social media post, a celebrant mentioned that he'd recently taken a funeral service for a ninety-four-year-old man who'd been a poacher and shooter all his life and, during the eulogy, the dear departed's son recalled eating roast curlew as a result. Prompted by this recollection, the celebrant asked 'what's the most unusual thing you've ever eaten' — and, irrespective of the legalities or otherwise, received the following replies!

I used to eat curlew. It was a nice meat, a bit salty for some people. I can still call them in, but obviously, I haven't shot them since they put them on the protected list.

My Dad as a lad ate rook pie, squirrel pie, starling pie, sparrow pie ... and hedgehog in clay wrapped in tin foil .When you fetched the clay off, it pulled the spines off ... his family used to live off the land ... They would trade meat for vegetables, i.e.; five starlings for potatoes ...

Wild boar brain.

I shot a lapwing when I was a kid and my dad said: 'You shot it, now you can eat it.' Was quite nice ...

Not quite so pleasant apparently, was this experience:

Ate a heron I shot when I was about ten — it was absolutely horrible.

BRAGGING RIGHTS

Lead shot worries

There is, in some quarters, concern about the effect of eating game shot and which may, as a result, contain lead pellets. In fact, there's been much scaremongering by those who would have shooting banned for whatever reason.

Mostly their arguments have been concerned with the possible danger to the health of those who eat shot game – or who buy it from the supermarkets that choose to stock it and, in July 2016, the then Secretary of State helped to put the record straight by confirming that: 'The Food Standards Agency (FSA) [had] sought independent scientific advice from the Committee on Toxicity about the human health risk,' as a result of which, the FSA maintained its existing opinion, which has been in place since 2012, remained relevant:

To minimise the risk of lead intake, people who frequently eat lead-shot game, particularly small game, should cut down their consumption. This advice is especially important for vulnerable groups such as toddlers and children, pregnant women and women trying for a baby.

Although a 1925 work of fiction by author John Buchan, several people have, over the years, claimed to have been the real-life inspiration for the book *John McNab*. Around the time of its publication, a certain J. E. Marriat-Ferguson claimed his grandparents knew Buchan's grandparents and that the two of them spent long periods fishing together in the Scottish Borders before both being called to the bar in the same year — and that he was the main character. Having said that, on another occasion, Marriat-Ferguson had also suggested he was a character in John Buchan's 1910 novel, *Prester John*, where the action focuses on South Africa. Whilst Marriat-Ferguson was undoubtedly present at every location during the right period, there's little, if any, documented evidence of either of his claims.

Far more credible is the letter to *The Field* magazine in 1951, written by Captain James Brander Dunbar, who insisted on bragging rights due to the fact that, many years before, he had claimed he could 'kill a beast in any forest in Scotland' without being detected by stalkers, ghillies or keepers. His claim being challenged — and subsequently put to the test — the captain seemingly won his bet.

NB: Apparently (and according to later correspondence), after the book was published, Buchan wrote to Brander apologising for failing to ask his permission to use the story.

Doing a 'McNab'

As a result of Buchan's book (which greatly expanded on the deer-stalking theme), a 'McNab' involves the challenge of taking a stag, a salmon and a brace of grouse — all within the space of twenty-four hours. All these years later, *The Field* magazine still retains an interest in such competition; as do several commercial sporting agencies. Nowadays, however, the requirement to poach, and remain undetected, is removed (and indeed, very much frowned upon) and all participants must have definite permission from the landowner and/or tenant.

NB: Regional 'McNabs' involving deer, fish, and game bird species most likely to be encountered in a particular area, also exist.

'Mine's bigger than yours'

Bragging rights can take many forms – but it has to be remembered that it's far better to let others notice and broadcast your particular prowess than to draw their attention to it by boasting: 'Did you see that high bird I took clean as a whistle ...?'

However, in America, it seems that shooting modesty is not required and, in some regions, shooting clubs even hold 'Bragging Rights Breakfasts' whereby solo hunters all join up and tell each other of their personal biggest and best achievements out on the shooting field.

I DON'T BELIEVE IT!

Whilst not quite claiming 'bragging rights', unless, that is, you're proud of getting money from an insurance company – which as we all know, are notorious for not paying out – these animal-related claims to the specialist insurance provider RIAS are well worth noting.

- A woman from Bath in Somerset, received a payout after locking a badger in her shed, which then ate a hole in the wall to escape.

- One family received a whopping £8,000 payout after a pigeon flew down their chimney and damaged the carpet, ornaments and sofas.

- A seven-month-old puppy in Cardiff caused £953 of damage when he pinched a bottle of oil from the kitchen, dragged it to the living room and chewed it while sitting on the couch.

- In Exeter, Devon, a squirrel smashed a window of an eighty-six-year-old woman after it became stuck in her garage.

- After seeing a dog on the TV, a dog in Galashiels tried to jump into the screen after it.

- A deer fell into the swimming pool of a seventy-four-year-old man from Guildford, damaging the cover.

What to Wear

There's many a myth regarding the origins of country clothing, which is, at least according to *Wikipedia*, that font of all knowledge:

> ... the traditional attire worn by men and women in rural Britain; it is the choice of clothing when taking part in outdoor sports such as equestrian pursuits, shooting, fishing, and during general outdoor activity such as when working outdoors, on picnics, walking, and gardening. It is also worn at events such as horse races, country weddings, beer festivals and country fairs.
>
> The form of dress although worn throughout Britain is mostly associated with England and is sometimes considered an historical form of dress or national costume, often worn to represent the English gentleman and lady. It is still considered countryside leisure wear and due to the durable, practical, comfortable and fashionable style, some people choose to use elements of country clothing for general usage in Britain.

Ah — so now we know!

THE TRUTH ABOUT TWEED

John Buchan's characters in *John McNab* (mentioned at the end of the last chapter) would, even though poaching, have almost certainly worn tweed. Even though there might be more practical and more modern alternatives available when it comes to clothing, if I'm a typical example then, whilst we wear the latest and most weatherproof clothing, there's still a reluctance to throw away that old tweed jacket hanging behind the door!

Known in the Scottish Highlands long before it became a useful material for a shooting suit, tweed is no longer the sole prerogative of the 'country set'. Today's tweed is sharp and sophisticated, oozes urban chic and glamour – and is just as likely to be seen on the High Street as it is up a High Seat. It's sturdy, comfortable, natural, and in most cases utterly indestructible. It is ethical, eco-friendly and naturally occurring: no wonder then that almost every clothing company in the world has tried – and failed – to create fabrics that imitate this perfectly imperfect fabric.

One popular misconception regarding tweed is that it is named after the river – which makes its way from Tweedsmuir through to the Scottish Borders, but it is not. Scottish tweed in fact originates from the far north-west (and other tweeds are available!).

Dyed in the wool

No matter how or where you intend wearing it, tweed is unquestionably one of the most interesting man-made fabrics you can ever imagine. In the main, hand-crafted and hand woven, tweed has occasionally been called the 'champagne of fabrics': its origins are, though, more that of a pint of beer. Made from rough, woven wool, according to the Harris Tweed Authority website: 'Crofters used a variety of vegetable dyes to colour the wool but perhaps the most popular used was the lichen Crotal (genus Parmelia), which was scraped from the plentiful rocks in the area. It produced a reddish brown colour, but the depth of colour depended on the quantity of crotal.'

Tweed is ethical, eco-friendly and naturally occurring

Sometimes the lichen was soaked for days in a warm solution of ammonia or alternatively a splash of what was euphemistically known as 'home solution', but was in fact urine, helped hold the colours in the cloth. The solution was then boiled under constant supervision for hours over a peat fire at the side of a stream or loch — all of which might help explain why, when traditional tweed gets wet it gives off an indescribable smell; somewhat akin to the smell your wet and woolly Springer spaniel might emit as it dries off in front of the fire!

Due in part to the natural weatherproofing already contained within the wool, tweed can be remarkably waterproof. Some say that tweed keeps the wearer even warmer when it gets wet because of the oil content in the weave and claim that 'it works a bit like a wetsuit'.

Types of tweed

When they think of tweed most think of the aforementioned Harris Tweed but there are other types: Welsh twills, Donegal tweeds, plain-cloth wool (from the west of England), cashmere, and even silk tweed. Interestingly, tweed designs are constantly changing as, with it being a natural product, the wool used varies from year to year.

On some shoots can be seen tweed wearers with a check and pattern so loud that it hits the onlooker straight between the eyes and gives them an instant migraine, but it's all a matter of suitability (forgive the pun) when it comes down to a colour and choice of check.

Intended originally to blend into the topography in which it is most likely to be worn, what looks 'loud' on a pheasant shoot in West Sussex can be quite literally lost when worn against a Highland backdrop. At least one Scottish landowner used to choose the tweed for his stalkers, keepers and ghillies by lining up a selection of possible cloth samples in the far distance before then 'glassing' them through a telescope in order to pick out the least obvious!

Tweed TLC

Some will glibly mention that the tweed suit, jacket or shooting coat originally belonged to their great-grandfather – and has been handed down. Don't dismiss this as a fabrication because it could so easily be true. As designer Eloise Grey says: 'Wear your garment year after year and hand it on.'

Over the years, tweed ages naturally – and with dignity. It resists water and dirt and is low on maintenance. Occasionally; however, it requires a little 'TLC'. There are several alternatives: you could, for instance, do as hunting folk do with their jackets and gently sponge or scrub any dirt-affected areas with clean rain water before allowing the garment to dry naturally. Dry it flat on a couple of deep-pile bath towels (pat it dry with a third towel): it's best not to hang it to 'drip-dry' as it could lose shape and the seams stretch. Under no circumstances try to wring it dry — you'll probably break your wrists with the effort and damage the weave into the bargain.

FULL NORFOLK JACKET

It's commonly thought that the Norfolk jacket was originally developed from a coat styled for hunting in the mid-1800s and many claim its 'inventor' to be Henry Fitzalan-Howard, 15th Duke of Norfolk: others attribute it to the Earl of Leicester, whose family seat is Holkham Hall, in Norfolk. According to some, the origins of the bowler hat is also reckoned to be Holkham — where it was developed as protective headgear for the estates' gamekeepers.

'Vintage' or simply second-hand?

It's long been considered that sportsmen and women are judged by the clothes they wear and the equipment they use – the general principal being the older, the better as such things denote experience and tradition. There's undoubtedly a ready market for such things at sporting auctions, on eBay and anywhere else where field sports enthusiasts might choose to look. One should, however, be aware of the difference between 'vintage' and second-hand.

Those in the know have it that vintage means that an item is not just 'old', it should have provenance and be clearly attributed to its maker, or even whoever (of note or otherwise) previously owned it. Second-hand (on the other hand!) items, do not have provenance; they are simply pre-owned – as one person put it: '... they are "ordinary" brands. Useful and good value, but minus the magic.'

If the latter is the case, then the Norfolk jacket (or something akin to it) has been around since the 1820s when, according to *The Gentleman's Gazette*: 'The Earl and his friends supposedly adopted the belted jacket with box pleats and roomy patch pockets, so they could conveniently carry all kinds of hunting accouterments. They opted for a belt — it improved the silhouette due to the snug fit and kept the cold air out.'

Whatever the truth, it soon 'became a wardrobe staple for well-dressed gentlemen' and was a jacket 'especially suited for bicycling, business, fishing, pleasuring, and the moorland' (*Tailor and Cutter*, April 1888).

Hands up

Single breasted with three or four front buttons, pleats and a full belt, the box pleats that, together with the all-round belt, make the Norfolk so recognisable, allow for greater arm movement that is so necessary when raising a gun to the shoulder. Sometimes the shoulders are enforced with a second layer of cloth or a leather patch; the vent is centred and the buttons are traditionally of leather, wood or deer horn. The pockets are expandable so as to hold cartridges and be able to gain quick, easy access to them.

Traditionally made from tweed, the Norfolk jacket has gone out of favour with many of today's Guns and field sports followers, mainly due to other lighter, more waterproof and easily cared-for items of shooting attire being so readily available.

THIS? ... I'VE HAD IT FOR AGES!

Warmth, flexibility and concealment are key qualities to consider when buying sporting clothes. Many people first took to the field in their childhood, dressed in a waxed coat teamed with black gumboots ... but on a cold, wet day the jacket became so stiff it was akin to wearing a straitjacket and the boots did nothing to keep the feet warm. How times change; there's now so much on offer that it can, at times, be quite bewildering.

As we've already seen earlier in this chapter, it's a tradition that whatever you wear shouldn't look new – as further evidenced by Gerald Warner, writing in *The Telegraph* in August 2008:

> A novice kitted out in brand-new knickerbockers and deerstalker might as well wear one of those conference badges saying 'Hedge fund manager'. A gentleman will be wearing tweeds weathered to the same consistency as the suit of armour his ancestor wore at Agincourt.
>
> If he has been obliged to replace his Barbour since last season, he may take the precaution of driving his tractor over it several times. Nor should the olfactory sense be neglected: if you cannot out-stink the wet gun dogs, your bona fides may be suspect.

It's a fact that, even if you want to carry off a look that suggests you've been shooting since the Year Dot, you should wear modern ear protection to keep you safe.

CLOTHING FOR THE EARS

Scientists have proven that it takes very little 'sonic trauma' to cause permanent damage and that for every five years of recreational shooting a person enjoys, the risk of high-frequency hearing loss escalates by some seven per cent.

The reasons given are, apparently, all to do with the cochlea — a fluid-filled, snail shell-shaped organ buried deep in the inner ear. Sound travels through the air as pressure waves and these are then directed down the ear canal to the eardrum, which vibrates. Its slight movements are relayed via three miniature bones (the hammer, stirrup, and anvil) to another membrane that covers the opening of the cochlea.

When this membrane begins to dance, the vibrations are transmitted inside the cochlea's fluid-filled centre, which is lined with minuscule hair-like projections called cilia that are adversely affected by high-frequency sounds. Intense noise, such as a shotgun blast, can cause vibrations so violent that they can, in effect, fell the affected cilia like an earthquake does trees.

Although impossible to totally eliminate the sound of gunshot, you can reduce it to a safer level — apparently and according to researchers, approximately 80 decibels — by the use of well-designed ear defenders, or even custom-fitted earplugs.

CLAY-BUSTING FAUX PAX

Ear protection is vital for the clay shooter. What he or she wears is, however, likely to be less formal than on some game shoots. Comfort and ease of swing is paramount but, despite what you might see at some clay shooting venues, there is still a need for decorum! An online blog suggests what *not* to wear:

Vests
Camouflage kit
Lycra leggings/cycling shorts Yoga/workout outfits
Colourful patterned shirts/shorts/skirts T-shirts with slogans
Cut-off jeans

What they wear is likely to be less formal...

BEST FOOT FORWARD

Did the Earl of Sandwich really invent the sandwich because he got a bit peckish but didn't want to leave the card table because he was on a winning streak — and so had a man-servant place a piece of meat between two slices of bread? (Apparently he didn't and research tells us that the concept of a sandwich was in hand long before the card-toting lord was a twinkle in his aristocratic father's eye). Did Lord Cardigan invent the cardigan (not in its present form, he didn't) and was the Duke of Wellington responsible for the invention of the Wellington boot?

As far as the latter is concerned, the answer has to be, 'sort of'. Wellington's boots were modified standard eighteenth-century hessian boots that were already in common usage. Adapted by his boot-maker, Mr Hoby, Wellington's were made in soft calfskin leather, cut close around the leg — and had low heels so as not to be an encumbrance in the stirrups when riding. They were then both stylish and hard-wearing.

Only when it became possible to vulcanise rubber was it possible to create the style of Wellington boot we all know and wear today. As Peter Holt points out in his book, *The Keen Countryman's Miscellany* (Quiller, 2012): 'The rubber version of the boot was created by Victorian entrepreneur Henry Lee Norris who, in 1856, launched the North British Rubber Company at a factory in Edinburgh. This subsequently became the Hunter Rubber Company, makers of Hunter gumboots.'

Fit for a princess

Ankle boots might suffice in some quarters when on the grouse moors or early season partridge shooting — or, unlikely for the majority — when one has someone else responsible for cleaning them in the manner of *Downton Abbey*. For most, though, it comes down to the Wellington type.

Journalist Harry Wallop began his *Daily Telegraph* article of 1 September 2015 (it being the start of the partridge shooting season) by asking whether there was ever 'an item of clothing more loaded with class assumptions than the Wellington boot?' and went on to opine that: 'The flat cap [and] tweed jacket ... are able to put a toe across Britain's social fault lines. But a pair of rubber boots designed to keep the rain from your feet says more about you than the school you attended ...'

Furthermore, he decided that: 'Hunters are no longer posh. They are plain naff,' and then commented that: 'Their place in the affections of the mwah-mwah brigade has been taken by a bewildering array of boots, all of which have subtle different class connotations.' Admiring and praising of the quality of 'Le Chameau' boots, he did, though, go on to suggest that their success was much to do with the patronage of the Duchess of Cambridge — as, or so he thought, was the similar popularity of the Hunter boot because of its wearing by Princess Diana and the 'Sloane Rangers' of the 1980s.

Old Wives' Tales

M any Guns have their own pet beliefs when it comes to avoiding discomfort during a shooting day – and not just with regards to clothing as has just been discussed in the preceding chapter. On the grouse moors, or on an early season partridge day, for example, you are likely to be accompanied by midges. Ideas as to how to rid oneself from their unwanted, unbridled embrace vary from the technical, to those of the old wives' variety – the latter of which range from the well-known, but unfortunately erroneous, idea that the smoke from cigarettes or cigars will keep them away, to eating copious amounts of Marmite, which, once exuded through the pores of your skin, midges apparently find repulsive.

MIDGES ON THE MOOR

What myths surround the midge – and what discomfort they can cause on the moorlands of Scotland in August when out grouse shooting or stalking. As one visiting stalker remarked: 'You need to go and experience them to understand just how bad they can be. More than once I've given up and headed southwards home as I couldn't cope with them anymore!' What facts and fallacies they engender too! What is known is that it's only the female midge that bites and swarms in high clouds — the less blood-thirsty males are happy to feed on nectar and lead a far more sedentary life. They don't, though, fly in wind speeds more than around 10mph and don't like it when the humidity level is below 60–75 per cent. They are seemingly more attracted to dark clothing than they are light colours — which is, I suppose, not very good news for deer stalkers

Midges on the moor

out on the hill. Nor, for that matter is the fact that they are particularly attracted to sweaty or unwashed clothing. The evil little things rarely fly above 3m from the ground and they bite more when they are flying low. They mainly bite near their breeding ground as the females go and pick a mate from a cloud of males — and they are almost always near a water source.

It's the opinion of many that most midge repellents don't work — or are at least of limited effectiveness. There are several options: DEET, citronella and Jungle Formula to name just some; however, the majority of those with most midge experience claim that Avon's 'Skin So Soft' dry oil body spray is the best deterrent — but warn that, on a sunny day (and yes, they do occur, even in Scotland!), you should first apply sunscreen as, it being oil-based, there's a chance of burning in strong sunlight.

A flea in sheep's clothing!

Old wives' tales have long had it that a fox will take a piece of sheep's wool from the field, hold it in its mouth and walk into water in order to rid itself of fleas (the parasites are supposed to move from the body as it immerses in water and run to the driest point – the sheep's wool – the fox then releases the wool together with its covering of fleas!). Sadly, no modern-day naturalist or scientist has ever proven this 'fact'.

RESPECT YOUR ELDER(S)

In days long gone, the German sportsman and countryman showed a deep reverence for their trees and would, before breaking off a branch (perhaps to place over a deer's body or in their mouth — *see* 'COUNTING THE BAG — EUROPEAN STYLE'), ask permission to do so from one of the many forest spirits — any one of which could be either beneficent or malevolent.

Bearing this in mind, before considering any habitat improvement on the shoot, particularly if elder is involved, it might pay to be aware of the following.

In the elder bush or tree supposedly lives the *Hylde-moer* (Elder-mother), who avenges each and every injury done to one of her trees – and so, on no account, at least according to the German legend, must any branches be cut until her permission has been sought. In Lower Saxony, the woodman would, on bended knee, ask permission by repeating three times, the incantation: 'Lady Elder, give me some of thy wood; then I will give thee, some of mine when it grows in the forest.' And all that with not as much as a 'please' and 'thank-you' ... terrible manners these Germans of old!

NB: According to more general folklore and custom, it is also unlucky to bring elder into the house for burning – as evidenced by the following lines taken from *The Firewood Poem* by Celia Congreve (which appears in full under 'A KNOTTY PROBLEM'): 'Make a fire of Elder tree, Death within your house will be.' You can't say you haven't been warned!

'To sleep; perchance to dream ...'

No gamekeeper in the Lincolnshire fields would ever dream of spending his lunch break under the boughs of an elder. In that particular part of the world, the leaves were thought to give off an aroma that, if inhaled for any length of time would, according to Steve Proud writing in *The Penguin Guide to the Superstitions of Britain and Ireland*, send the recumbent into a coma – from which he might never awake.

Likewise, a 1905 newspaper account from the next door county went as follows:

A few days ago a gamekeeper ... was chasing some fowls from a spinney to the roost, when he tripped up on an elder-bush, a spike of which entered his hand. It is a popular superstition that a wound from the elder is fatal, and it proved so in this case. The wound was promptly dressed, and an operation performed a few days later at Cambridge Hospital, but he died in that institution yesterday from tetanus.

'GO TELL THE BIRDS AND BEES'

An old traditional British custom, 'telling the bees' of a birth, marriage or death used to be commonplace at a time when many households had their own beehive. The practice is well-known, especially when involving the death of a family member. Far less well-known is the rural practice and tradition of 'telling the rooks'. In fact, despite having done considerable research as a result of being told about the custom by an old north Lincolnshire gamekeeper many years ago, the only written reference I can find to it is in a magazine article published in the early 1950s:

> A noisy colony of rooks occupied a plantation near the house, and tradition demanded that on the first dawn after a birth or death it was the duty of the head of the house, or the eldest member of the family present, to announce the fact beneath the trees before the birds had left on their foraging for food.
>
> In a small recess just inside the hall door was kept the 'rook bell', similar to a sheep bell but with a short handle instead of a leather thong. The bell had to be rung vigorously before any announcement was made.

At Newstead Abbey, Nottinghamshire, nearby residents had it that the rooks living in the grounds were the souls of the 'Black Monks' still occupying their old abbey and, as such (as in north Lincolnshire), were left unhindered; contrary to common country practice in the majority of rural Britain.

'My Kingdom for a ... crow!'

In centuries gone by, certain birds, particularly those of the corvid family, were thought of as being bringers of ill fortune. Even as far back as Shakespeare's time, 'magot-pies and choughs' encouraged (in *Macbeth*) man's lust for blood, whilst in *Julius Caesar* it was mentioned that any 'crows and kites' seen overhead would indicate a defeat in battle.

'MORNING MR MAGPIE'

The bane of both shooting estates and suburban gardens due to its propensity to take game and songbird eggs and chicks, the magpie is much loathed by many. There's also a great deal of superstition attached to its presence.

Most of us know the rhyme, 'one for sorrow, two for joy' — and some of us (when minus a gun and out on a walk), might even doff our caps on seeing a magpie cross the track and call out, 'Good morning Mr Magpie. How is your lady wife today?' Why do we do so when, as we've already seen, magpies are an unwelcome presence on the shoot?

Well, in most parts of the United Kingdom spying a single magpie is considered an omen of bad fortune and saluting it is a way of showing the proper respect in the hope that the magpie won't pass on some of the misfortune that follows it. As to the rhyme, its origins could well be based on the belief that magpies mate for life and seeing one on its own is a sign of sorrow because it's lost its mate — whereas if two are seen, it's assumed that they are a pair and one is supposed to be joyful about their relationship.

Despite the continued efforts of gamekeepers and their springtime use of Larsen traps, magpie numbers remain at least constant, if not on the increase. Various theories for the increase include the supposition that, until relatively

recently (in the scale of things), their numbers were kept in check by the relative lack of food during the winter and early spring. Nowadays, some would have it that it's the increase in the number of cars on the roads that has led to a corresponding increase in wildlife road casualties – a situation of which scavenging magpies take full advantage.

Not a lot of people know that!

Apparently, the Latin word for magpie – *Pica* – is also the term for a strange psychological disorder known as 'Pica Syndrome' whereby sufferers eat non-nutritive substances as bizarre as nails, glass and buttons. The origins of the medical term is derived from the magpie's propensity to collect, and sometimes eat, almost anything, particularly if it's at all shiny.

RESPECT

While there's the occasional countryman that will doff his or her hat to a magpie, there's many more that will lift his hat to a fox or hare as he sees it pass by. I've seen it often when a hunting person who also shoots is standing by a peg waiting for the first birds of the drive to fly over and the noise of the beaters has pushed a fox or hare forward.

Even when, at the pre-shoot talk, the host has given permission for a fox or hare to be taken ('Provided it's a safe shot'), many decline out of respect for an animal that, in their opinion – and as a result of tradition that goes long beyond the 2004 Hunting Act – is a far better quarry hunted than it is shot.

OUT FOR A DUCK

Can a fox walk under a roosting pheasant and mesmerise it so much that it drops from the tree and provide an easy meal, as so many old wife's tales maintain?

Probably not — but what is true is the fact that, in days gone by, a trained dog could so attract the attention of wild ducks that they would swim after it as it ran along the bank and follow it straight into the specially constructed decoy pens of Dutch (and subsequently, East Anglian) professional duck decoyers.

Large numbers of duck could be caught in one 'hit' by such methods. Probably the most famous one in the UK is the Boarstall Decoy in Buckinghamshire, which is now owned by the National Trust, but records still in existence at the Hale Decoy in Cheshire indicate that catches of more than 400 ducks per year were common there. These were mainly mallard, wigeon and teal. The largest catch was 1,162 in 1875.

Complicated and clever, a decoy might involve a tree-sheltered pond on to which duck numbers would regularly pitch for food provided by the decoyman or estate gamekeeper (quite often one and the same). 'Pipes' (in reality, metal-hooped and netting-clad tunnels), radiated out from the pond and were about 50 yards in length. At the edge of the pond their height might have been around 12ft and their typical width about 20ft but, as the pipe progressed away from the pond, they tapered down dramatically.

Along the outer curve of each pipe were erected wooden screens; which were erected in such a way that the decoyman could move about unseen. More importantly, they allowed his trained dog to slip in and out between them in a 'now you see, me, now you don't' sort of way — an action that was crucial in drawing the inquisitive ducks towards the narrow end of the pipes where they could more easily be captured.

He who pays the piper

The breed of dogs used to decoy the ducks were many and varied: generally, though, they were of a type bred specifically for the purpose; today, perhaps the two most well-known ones are the Kooikerhondje from Holland and the Nova Scotia Toller (aka Nova Scotia Duck Tolling Retriever) which, as its name suggests, originates from Canada.

Most were predominantly 'red' or fox-brown in colour (so perhaps there is

something in the old wives' tale of a fox being able to mesmerise a roosting pheasant after all?) and traditionally, they were quite often given the name of 'Piper'. In his online article, *Recalling the Red Decoy Dog*, writer and working dog aficionado Col David Hancock mentions that collie-sized dogs were often used for the job and that: 'Throw-backs to this collie-like red-coated lavishly-tailed clever agile dog still occur in country areas; their luxuriantly furnished tails are flourished exorbitantly when alert to feathered game.'

A HARD TALE TO SWALLOW

For centuries, due to the fact that they were continually seen skimming over the surface and then, at a given point of the year, suddenly disappeared, many country folk thought that swallows 'flew' to the bottom of ponds and hibernated there throughout winter.

Not always known for its accuracy, *Wikipedia* nevertheless has this information concerning the subject — particularly as it pertains to eighteenth-century naturalist Rev Gilbert White and his book, *The Natural History of Selborne*:

First published in 1789 by Benjamin White (Gilbert's brother), the book has not been out of print [since] ... White is recognised as being the first ecologist or environmentalist [and] most of his observations on wildlife remain pertinent, although he did have some strange theories; most notorious is his belief that not all swallows, martins and swifts migrated, but that some might hibernate instead, although he mocked the peculiar Swedish notion that swallows spent the winter beneath the surface of the local ponds ...

It must, however, be remembered that Gilbert White was writing his notes and observations before seasonal migration was fully understood and therefore kept his options open; even to the extent of paying farm labourers to dig around in the bottom of ponds and other likely 'hibernating' spots just in case!

A LOTTA BOTTLE

In his *A Gamekeeper's Notebook* (1910), Owen Jones tells his readers that North Country poachers trapped grouse alive by pressing a bottle into hard snow and shaping a hole into which the grouse falls head-first, reaching after corn at the bottom, and from which it cannot escape.

One can't help but wonder whether the writer had been at the contents of the aforementioned bottle; firstly because grouse do not eat corn and, secondly, how deep would the snow have to be in order that the bird could not fly and scramble out?

BLACKBERRY FOOL

Whilst you are standing at your peg in late September or early October waiting for partridges to come winging their way towards you, you might be tempted to forage a nearby hedge in search of juicy blackberries — but be warned! According to tradition, you should never eat them after Michaelmas Day (29 September), 'for they will have the Devil in them'. Superstition it may be but there is an element of truth in the old saying because, by then, many blackberries will be past their best.

RABBITTING ON

Whilst it's obviously not so lucky for the poor creature from whence it came, there's long been a tradition that carrying a rabbit's foot in your pocket will bring luck.

The Celts, by around 600 BC, are known to have associated rabbits with good fortune — the whole rabbit, not just the foot. According to their beliefs, the fact that rabbits lived in burrows deep underground meant that they were in direct communication with the spirits of the underworld.

Rabbits are also connected to health and fecundity. By the sixteenth century it was thought that carrying a rabbit's foot around would ease the pain of arthritis whilst, should you be wishing for a son and heir to carry on the family name and continue the estate management, a rabbit's foot about your person was a sure aid to fertility. An unsurprising connection really, considering that rabbits breed ... well ... just like rabbits!

FRENCH FOOLISHNESS

Many British field sports enthusiasts regularly pop across the water to enjoy their chosen sport. Just to be sure you don't put your foot in it whilst doing so, here are a few superstitions particular to France.

Putting your foot in it

If you quite literally 'put your foot in it', you can – so it seems – expect good luck in whatever it is you're doing that day. Apparently, if you step in dog excrement with your left foot, all will be well: your game bag or fishing creel will be full or, if you are out riding to hounds, an excellent day's sport will be had. Bearing in mind that, in the former and latter scenarios, dogs are likely to feature quite highly, good luck might reasonably be assumed ... but remember, it must be your left foot that treads in the offending mess; if it's the right, your day's sport is presumably doomed!

The staff of life

If you are ever asked out beating on a shoot in France and get reminded 'not to forget your baguette', you are not necessarily being told about lunchtime arrangements – the French word for a walking stick (used for beating or otherwise) is a 'baguette' ... but the name is also used to describe a type of long, thin French loaf.

Once that possible *faux pas* is sorted, you need to know how to handle your bread if you want to avoid bad luck. Never place a baguette or a loaf of bread on a table upside down as, according to folklore, there's a good chance that, if you do, both you and the other people the bread is intended to feed will suffer from a 'hunger curse' – a situation no self-respecting food and wine-loving French person could ever tolerate!

Strike a light

After the shoot lunch, it might be time to get out the cigars. A 'good' cigar should always be lit with a match and never a cigarette lighter as to do so risks contaminating the cigar's flavour.

Neither is lighting one with a match without potential hazard: it's considered bad luck to try and light three cigars (or cigarettes) with the same match.

Whilst it's a superstition common to other countries, it actually stems from the World War One battlefields of France where, in the trenches, lighting one cigarette with a match may have alerted a German sniper; lighting a second would let the sniper know how far away the enemy is and, doing the same to a third, was likely to mean that the recipient of such kindness would be the one to be shot.

Should you be at the kind of upmarket shoot dinner where such things adorn the table, never light your cigar or cigarette from a candle. Seemingly, if you do, a sailor at sea will drown – or at least lose their job. Deliberately lighting a cigarette from a candle purely in order to get back at the rude barman or ferry company employee that you encountered whilst on the journey over the English Channel will not, however, necessarily bring about their comeuppance!

The owl and the pussy cat

Throughout much of the world, countrymen and women have often treated owls with suspicion but, according to French custom at least, they can be a useful ally if you and your partner are expecting a baby and are possibly hoping for a girl. If a woman sees an owl during any of the nine months she is pregnant then she is practically guaranteed to have one. Don't actively seek out a barn owl, though: sighting one of these in or around your home is, like the tortoiseshell cat below, a bad omen.

Feral felines

Feral cats are rarely welcomed on any shoots where the rearing of wild game is encouraged but, tempted though they may be to try and eradicate the problem one way or the other, French gamekeepers (*garde de chasse*) are advised to take care when encountering a cat on the land for which they are responsible.

Unlike in Britain where seeing a black cat is considered good luck, in France exactly the opposite is true. Likewise, never cross a French stream whilst holding a cat in your arms and, if in Normandy, it's to be hoped you never see a tortoiseshell cat as doing so is said to 'foretell your death in an accident'.

Horsing around

Many shoots in the UK have, as their meeting point, a set of outbuildings and, over the door of at least one of them, you are almost certain to see an old horseshoe hanging for good luck. The iron it contains is said to ward off evil spirits but it should always be hung with the gap to the top otherwise all the good luck will run out of it. Not so in France and, should you ever be charged with placing a horseshoe in a similar position, it must be placed upside down.

NB: Horseshoes are, as you know, commonly used as a symbol of good luck at weddings – and are supposed to protect the bride and groom from the Devil's power. This originates from the legend of how, when the Devil asked St Dunstan to shoe his cloven hooves, the not-so-saintly Saint purposefully hurt him. In exchange for mercy, the Devil promised never to enter any place where a horseshoe (hanging either up or down) is displayed.

NOT IN MY HOUSE

Sometimes things happen that you cannot avoid – such as a robin entering through an open window. However, countryside superstition has it that a robin in the house is a portent of death. As I noted in my book, *Curious Country Customs* (David & Charles, 2007): 'On Dartmoor, this superstition was taken to such an extreme that if you received a Christmas card portraying a robin, you were supposed to rip it up immediately, as it meant that the sender was wishing you bad luck.'

What's that smell?

Similar dire consequences might occur if you bring the flowers of either lilac or hawthorn into the house – hawthorn is one of the sacred trees of witchcraft, and lilac was used to line coffins to mask the odour of death.

It's My Delight

Weather and the moon (think duck-flighting when connecting the two) affects a shooting day in many ways – the effects of certain climatic conditions as experienced by keepers trying to provide a good high bird, Guns attempting to shoot them and the difficulties the pickers-up may experience with scenting in any given weather, all have influence. It is, therefore, sometimes quite useful to know what the weather is likely to be doing. In this day and age, you can, of course, get a fairly accurate weather forecast from television, radio, the internet or a mobile phone 'app' – but what about some of the more traditional methods of weather-forecasting?

Countryside writer Robin Page gave an example of 'old weather lore being more accurate than modern forecasts when, in his book, *Weather Forecasting: The Country Way*, published in 1977, he opined that:

... towards the end of the famous and enjoyable drought of 1976 ... Because of the parched conditions, one water authority decided, at great cost, to follow the advice of 'experts' and made a large East Anglian river flow backwards. Wise countrymen shook their heads commenting 'The weather always equals itself out', and some men quoted the old saying:

'Be it dry or be it wet,
The weather will always pay its debt.'

As soon as the pumps were installed it began to rain. The drought was over, and an exceptionally wet winter followed.

RED SKY AT NIGHT

A piece of seaweed hanging at the back door works in the following, quite logical way: if it's moist and/or pliable to the touch, the air is probably humid, or a storm is approaching, but if it's dry and brittle, the weather is likely to be dry. Then there are also the old sayings such as 'red sky at night, shepherd's delight; red sky in the morning, shepherd's warning', and, to be a good natural weather forecaster, you really do need to be up as early as possible in the morning for it is the first few hours of the day that are most likely to indicate what's likely to follow.

In summer the early dew soaks the grass; in winter the grass and even the trees are white with frost. If the frost fades quickly, or there is no dew, a change is on the way. But if the day continues fine, the horizon not too sharp, the sky soft and the sun sinks in an even red glow, the fine weather will continue.

Watch the activities of the animals, birds and insects. Some can hear thunder long before humans can – a pheasant, for instance, will 'cock-up' at the first signs many miles away whilst bees become agitated and desperate to return to the hive. Many insects hatch in warm or humid weather and cattle on the run with their tails up are not frightened by an impending storm but more because of the warble flies, which hatch under such conditions. With a storm heading their way, many animals and birds become restless and, if of a certain ages, your rheumatic joints might begin to ache!

Red sky at night...

THE LINCOLNSHIRE POACHER

The Lincolnshire poacher most certainly got it wrong when he declared that:

When I was bound apprentice in famous Lincolnshire,
Full well I serv'd my master, for more than seven year,
Till I took up to poaching, as you shall quickly hear.
Oh, 'tis my delight on a shining night, in the season of the year.

A night where the moon is shining is one of the worst times to go out poaching. You might be able to see the pheasants in the trees but they can also see you — and will most likely clatter off the roost long before you're able to get near enough with your air rifles, catapult or whatever is your chosen weapon.

OCTOBER — AND THE HUNTER'S MOON

The 'Hunter's Moon' is the first full moon following the harvest moon of September; it rises around sunset, sets around sunrise and is the only point of the month when the moon is in the sky all night long — it did, at one time, indicate the start of the hunting season (and food in the winter larder) for our ancestors. The moon also has its fair share of weather predictions this month — a 'halo' around the moon has long been thought to be a portent of bad weather:

Rain in October
Gives wind in December.
If the October moon comes without frost,
Expect no frost until the moon of November

Alternatively:

> *If ducks do slide at Hallow-tide,*
> *At Christmas they do swim;*
> *If ducks do swim at Hallow-tide,*
> *At Christmas they will slide*

Many weather predictions for October seem to be based around birds; if, for example, fieldfares and redwings are seen this month, a hard winter is sure to follow. Tradition also has it that if a squirrel has a bushy tail, it indicates a cold snap: in reality, a bushy tail is an early warning system to other squirrels, but let's not let that fact spoil an old country maxim! Likewise, a plethora of fruits such as blackberries (and don't forget to pick them before the witches spit on them!) is said to indicate some inclement weather to come: botanic evidence proves that the amount of berries on a bush or tree depends entirely on the weather conditions during the preceding spring. And finally, for every fog in October, there will apparently be a snowfall in the winter.

FOGGY DAYS AND PIGEON

Denys Watkins-Pitchford ('B. B.') was of the opinion that: 'Foggy days are deadly for pigeon' ... and went on to explain that: 'Like most birds, geese included, they are quite lost in fog and will sit in the tree tops for hours together hunched and motionless.' Written in an article published some six decades ago, Watkin-Pitchford's observations are nevertheless verified by the experiences of others contributing to various online shooting forums a generation or more later.

All maintain that fog is the only time one can 'stalk' pigeons and get close enough to have any hope of a shot. Moreover, even when you have fired at one, the remainder will quite often mill around before dropping back into the same trees from which they were disturbed. When roost shooting, fog can also help as birds tend to come in low — as they do when decoying in (light) fog in situations where they can just make out your decoys.

Grandmother's footsteps

Even in foggy conditions, it will still pay to keep your movement to the minimum — and to play 'Grandmother's Footsteps' when trying to outwit pigeons along the hedgerows. World champion clay-shooter and keen pigeon shot, George Digweed, is on record as saying: 'Keeping still until the optimum moment when you are looking to take the shot is absolutely the key to success; movement, I think, is the biggest contributing factor to making the birds jink.'

Why won't my game crops grow?

Many gardeners believe in planting vegetables during specific phases of the moon – and there may be a case for similar thinking when it comes to the planting of game crops on the shoot. Too many accounts exist for the system to be pure fallacy and, whilst there is some disagreement as to the exact details, it is generally thought that planting when the moon is waxing ensures rapid germination and growth. Another idea is that types that grow underground (stubble turnips, for example) should be planted when the moon phase is at its darkest, and those that grow above ground (maize and similar) should be planted during a period of full moon.

BLACKTHORN WINTER

Blackthorn is easy to differentiate from hawthorn because of its darker bark — and because of its height: hawthorn frequently being as tall as 10m whereas the blackthorn rarely exceeds even half that height. The blackthorn also flowers earlier – and before it gets its summer leaves. Many myths surround the blackthorn and the ancients held it in great respect – and not just because of the sharpness of its thorns, which have been the undoing of many Guns and beaters as they struggle to squeeze through a hedgerow of it ... no wonder it is known as the 'snag-bush' by many.

Its thorns are, nonetheless, well worth tolerating in the autumn when the flowers of early spring have, over the summer, turned to small green berries – and then, in the autumn, sloes with which one can make all manner of things but, in the case of most of us, notably, sloe gin!

An unusual decoration

A farming tradition has it that hawthorn brings good luck and, for many years, in certain parts of the British Isles, it was a regular custom to drape the fresh placenta from a milking cow or working mare over a nearby hawthorn bush as it was thought that it would protect the newly calved/foaled mother from any illness that might otherwise occur after the birth.

THE WAY THE WIND BLOWS

In 1923, Ernest Ingersoll pointed out that there was still strong superstition and strange practices being carried out when it came to weather forecasting in general and wind direction in particular

— including the use of mummified kingfishers!

... I find many non-mythical notions, historical or existing, concerning the ... kingfisher ... One of the oldest is the custom formerly in vogue in England, and more recently in France, of turning this bird into a weathercock. The body of a mummified kingfisher with extended wings would be suspended by a thread, nicely balanced, in order to show the direction of the wind, as in that posture it would always

The way the wind blows

turn its beak, even when hung inside the house, toward the point of the compass whence the breeze blew. Kent, in *King Lear*, speaks of rogues who:

*'Turn their halcyon beaks
With every gale and vary of their masters.'*

And after Shakespeare, Marlowe, in his *Jew of Malta*, says:

*'But how stands the wind?
Into what corner peers my halcyon's bill?'*

We are told that the fishermen of the British and French coasts hang these kingfisher weathervanes in the rigging of their boats; and it seems likely to me that it was among sailors that the custom began.

WET OVER WILL'S MOTHER'S PLACE

Many regions of Britain have their own folklore attached to their particular area: for example: 'If you can't see the fells, it's raining; if you can see the fells, it's about to rain!' or: 'If you don't like the weather, just hang around ten minutes — it'll have changed by then.' Way back in 1699, John Worlidge noted in his tome, *Systema Agriculturae*, that:

If small black clouds appear on a clear evening, it means rain.
If during a cold, dry winter's day great black clouds come from the north and appear whitish when near to you, it signifies snow or hail.
If while the rain is lashing down the winds rise or fall, it signifies that the rain will stop.

Various regions have their own words for the weather too: in Staffordshire, for instance, the intense stillness and humidity immediately before a storm is sometimes referred to as 'puthery' whilst in Scotland, a squall accompanied by heavy rain is known as a 'blad'. If there's dull, low cloud and it's drizzly, it's 'dimpsey' in Devon and Cornwall, whilst if it's windy in Northumberland, it's 'gowsty'. From the same area comes 'plash'; used to denote a downpour — a phenomenon with which most of us involved in field sports of one sort or another are particularly familiar!

> **Rain before seven, fine before eleven**
>
> Apparently there's some truth in this: nonetheless, the Met Office warns that: 'As fronts pass at night as often as they do during the day, morning rain isn't always a predictor of a dry afternoon.' It will pay to pack your waterproofs!

READ THE SIGNS

Many things to do with flora and fauna are weather-related. A fact I've noticed whilst boar shooting in France is that, in the spring, if the pale brimstone butterfly appears early season after a spell of bad weather, several days of good weather will follow. As to whether or not there's any hard evidence to support my 'fact', I've yet to discover!

 In amongst all the superstition associated with the countryside, hornets have often been seen as foretellers of the likely weather. Such superstition created the old rhyme, 'If hornets build low/Winter storms and snow/If hornets build high/Winter mild and dry.'

Most probably, the rhyme was founded upon the belief that hornets remain in their nests during the winter, in which case they would be safer to build low when a hard season was at hand. A relevant website seems, in a way, to bear out this thinking:

Probably a truer prediction is that made by an observant gamekeeper who said that the height at which wasps make their nests above the water is a rough index of the amount of rain expected during the summer. In a wet season they choose the top of the bank near a brook, in dry they may build almost at the water's level.

 In the country, old sayings die hard. It's a sure sign that it's going to rain if you see swans flying — or so we are told. Noel M. Sedgwick ('Tower-Bird'), one time editor of *The Shooting Times*, had this comment to make in 1950:

It may be that swans are affected by atmospheric pressure. Most of us have seen rooks soaring high in the air and tumbling earthwards like so many leaves in a storm. But swans also fly for a reason which does not seem to strike the average countryman — to get from one place to another! If, and I rather doubt it, swans are encouraged to fly at times before impending rain, it does not take impending rain to make them fly.

 Countrymen have long held the view that cows and sheep lie down before rain — scientists tell us that, whilst there is no truth in this, it nevertheless seems to be a fact that they prefer laying in a south–north direction rather than west–east.

 In other situations (on a shooting day, for instance), watching a flock of sheep bunch together and looking towards a corner of their field can indicate that the beating team is just heading towards the first drive ... or that something untoward — like a straying dog — has just caught their attention.

An unusual amount of worm casts suddenly appearing on the stately home lawn was once said to be indicative of the arrival of migrant snipe – and caused the gentleman-shooter great excitement … at least according to Hugh B. C. Pollard (author of, amongst other things: *A History of Firearms; Game Birds and Game Bird Shooting* and *The Gun Room Guide*). Pollard was also of the opinion that whilst there were no real hard and fast rules likely to indicate a likely day for snipe, 'it is worth keeping an eye open for reports of "Ice in the Baltic" and other remote weather items.'

Woodcock and their annual migration are a source of fascination to most shooting people. Although still very much of a mystery, general opinion has it that they come in to the UK ahead of colder weather – and on a full moon in November or December. The GWCT's research on the subject provides some interesting actual facts and figures (*www.gwct.org.uk/research/species/birds/woodcock*).

The tracks of your deers!

Look out for any worn crossing points as it is quite likely they are made by deer or hares, the prints of which can often be easily seen. With experience, it is even possible to work out the individual deer species; roe have smaller, more closed hoof prints than do say, a fallow deer. Evidence of webbed feet will suggest wild duck – most likely mallard – and sprawled-out bird prints with just a touch of 'webbing' between them, either coots or moorhens. Pheasants like marshy areas and their chicken-like footprints are easy to spot. As otters are now known to frequent every county of the UK, it might even be possible to see their footprints in the mud. However, it is probably more likely that such prints were made by mink.

From tracks, you can learn a lot. It's possible to see what animals are about, where they come and go and the range of their wanderings. Richard Ford, writing for the *Country Fair* magazine in 1953, pointed out that: 'Animals often have one odd claw growing at a slightly abnormal angle or position, and from this you can pick out one animal from others of its kind and even recognise its tracks perhaps a year or so later.'

Watching Wildlife

A great part of the pleasure of shooting is the opportunity it offers to observe and learn – and watch the wildlife – whilst walking up a hedgerow, or standing on your peg at a driven shoot.

Not all that long ago, I was in Devon where I was supposed to be gathering material for an article dealing with working Sealyham terriers. The idea was for the pack and their huntsman to seek out rats, or maybe the odd rabbit or two (things nowadays being much curtailed since the *2004 Hunting Act*). In the event, any intended quarry eluded us but, during our time out, we saw much evidence of Dartmoor wildlife, both flora and fauna.

Native wild brown trout lazily fanned their tail fins to keep them in situ under the cover of the bank. A heron flew over; wagtails flittered from stone to stone – and we convinced ourselves that we'd seen a dipper. Chaffinches flew from wind-blown tree to tree, possibly in the hope of distracting us from a nearby nest, and an unusually coloured (fawn) wild duck clattered out from under the roots of an overhanging tree. On one of the raised stones, an otter had (very) recently left its calling card in the shape of a 'spraint'.

All of which goes to show what non-hunting people so very often fail to realise: the finding, hunting and killing of their possible quarry is of comparatively little consequence; it's the day out with like-minded people enjoying nature, and watching dogs or hounds proficient at their job, that is far more important.

WINTER WONDERLAND

Because of their field sports interests, there's many who prefer the winter to the summer, including E. M. Barraud who, in 1948, opined that:

It is as though in the skeleton of the trees and the bare outline of the winter scene you see the real essence of it all, stark, maybe, but basic. The winter landscape is fluid, translucent, limitless — all the spaciousness of the earth is in it. In a fully clothed summer landscape, lovely though it may be, there is that sense of being confined ... Summer fullness cloys but winter tang is always fresh and vital.

YEW HAD TO BE THERE!

Many years before shotguns and rifles, Man hunted his food with the aid of a bow and arrow. The English longbowmen became famous at the Battle of Agincourt (defeating the French with their new-fangled crossbows) both for their prowess and the supposed origins of the two-fingered salute (*see below*)!

Made of yew, the English longbow was unmatched because of the wood's flexibility and spring. Far earlier than that, yew made a more than suitable bow for ancient Britons (and also for the tips of hunting spears – as documented during the excavation of the 'Clacton spear tip' found in Essex in 1911 that supposedly dates to 400,000 BC).

Tradition has it that yews were grown in churchyards as, at the time they were planted, such places were the only areas likely to have been fenced and the trees thus protected against livestock. In reality, livestock tends to have an inherent knowledge that even a few mouthfuls of yew leaves could prove fatally poisonous and tend to steer well clear. Interestingly, though, deer and rabbits seem able to develop a resistance by continually eating small amounts. Where the theory breaks down somewhat is the fact that some ancient yews actually predate the churches and were planted in places considered sacred to pagans – upon which Christians then built their points of worship!

Yew trees have also been used as parish boundary markers over the years. In fact, in 2000, to help celebrate the Millennium, several parish councils – among them, Milland in West Sussex – planted more at strategic points. So, should you find yourself at a peg waiting for the first partridge or pheasant to come over; take a look around and see if there are any yews in the vicinity – and if there are, ponder on their age and previous importance to hunters of times passed.

Up yours!

Frequently used as a good-natured insult on many a shoot (well, it is on some of the ones with which I've been involved!), whilst the two-fingered salute is

Up yours!

said to have originated at the Battle of Agincourt (1415) as a result of gestures made by English longbow archers to their French crossbow-toting opposition, there appears to be no actual historical evidence to support the story.

In his book, *Gestures: Their Origins and Distribution* (1979), anthropologist, Desmond Morris studied the history and spread of European gestures and found the rude version of the V-sign to be basically unknown outside the

British Isles. Whilst coming to no definite conclusion, he had this to say: 'It is known to be "dirty" and is passed on from generation to generation by people who simply accept it as a recognised obscenity without bothering to analyse it ... Several of the rival claims are equally appealing. The truth is that we will probably never know ...'

BEECH BABES

As to other trees of the woodland, beech is apparently (and who decides these things?) associated with femininity and is often considered the queen of British trees (oak being considered the king). In Celtic mythology, 'Fagus' was the god of beech trees: the beech is also thought to have medicinal properties and its leaves have been used to relieve swellings or, after being boiled, to make a poultice suitable for either human or animal.

Should you happen to be looking for an underground water source on the shoot, forked beech twigs have long been traditionally used for divining.

In *A Gamekeeper's Handbook*, first published in 1954 by Gilbertson & Page, there's some very pertinent advice regarding sound carrying at night:

When watching at night do not forget that sound carries much farther on the still night air, a noise hardly discernable by day then being heard at a considerable distance. Above all things avoid communicating with a fellow watcher by means of what is known as a stage whisper, for this may often be heard farther than the voice in undertone. When moving from one position to another step very lightly and flat-footed, and do not drag the feet through herbage.

MINK MENACE

Sometimes whilst watching wildlife, one can come across the unexpected — and help cull the unwanted. Very few animals are as undesirable on the shoot as the American mink, which was introduced into Britain purely in order to be farmed for its fur.

Any efforts to get rid of this insidious menace has to be a good thing as they have done untold damage to native wild stocks of birds and animals throughout the whole of the UK since escaping or being deliberately released from mink farms by animal rights activists thirty years or so ago. They use small streams and ditches in order to travel to and fro and will, as they do so, predate on fish, many indigenous (and often rare) small mammals and the eggs, chicks and adults of waterfowl species — as well as decimating gamebird stocks, both wild and reared.

Be careful of what you wish for

I doubt you'd ever see mink advertised for sale nowadays — and yet, sixty years ago, they appeared quite frequently in the classified ads of the likes of *Country Life* and similar magazines. One such read: 'Mink from Britain's supreme herd of champion-bred standards ... largest in the UK. 2,000 minks. All equipment stocked. Free illustrated brochure — St Lawrence Mink Farm, Wolfcastle, Pembs.'

MUSICAL MUNTJAC

Imported from the Far East, muntjac deer were introduced to parks in the UK in the early twentieth century and escapees have since established wild populations. Relatively common in certain parts, they are rarely seen unless flushed out by the beaters on a shooting day, or observed by a stalker out at dawn and dusk after a roe deer or similar.

Their 'barking' is, however, very different to the call a roe deer might make – and as well as the repeated barking, an alarmed adult might scream, whereas maternal does and youngsters give out more of a squeak.

Molecular scientists are very enthusiastic about muntjac, as they – or rather their ancestors – have been around for millennia, (the species, that is, not the biologists) and are 'of great interest for their dramatic chromosome variations'.

THE CALL OF THE WILD

In Britain there are many animals and birds that will come to one call or another – a fact that could prove useful when 'squeaking' a fox or trying to attract the attention of a rutting deer ... some old keepers' tales should, however, be taken with that proverbial 'pinch of salt', particularly when it is suggested that it's possible to catch a rabbit by sprinkling pepper on a rock (the rabbits sneezes because of the pepper and knocks itself out on the rock!)

The highs and lows of a high seat

A high seat – primarily intended for deer shooting – is also the ideal location for predator control, wildlife observation and a whole host of other activities ... but which country first came up with the concept?

It's pretty safe to assume that the idea of high seats originated in Europe, where they've been used for deer management in large tracts of woodland for many years (was their construction and idea adapted by the Germans when they constructed their wartime 'goon towers'?). They are particularly invaluable on relatively flat topography, when to shoot from ground level could be pretty dangerous.

Whilst high seats might have been late arrivals to the British stalking scene, there was, nonetheless, something far more grandiose in existence long before then: the coursing grandstand, house-like buildings, from the top of which sportsmen (and women) of the day could watch as deer were driven past and then, when sufficient 'law' was given, greyhounds would be slipped in chase.

In John Nichol's *The Progresses and Public Processions of Queen Elizabeth*, written in 1823, the author mentions a royal visit to West Sussex: 'Then rode hir (sic) Grace to Cowdray to dinner, and about six of the clocke in the evening, from a turret, sawe sixteen buckes ... pulled down with greyhounds ...'

Whilst it's possible to buy squeakers and callers, it's also possible to make your own – or, in the case of needing to imitate a squealing rabbit or hare, simply suck on the back of one's hand in order to make an appropriate noise. Whatever you use, it's necessary to keep out of sight, or at least perfectly still, and use the wind intelligently.

Stoats and weasels will be attracted by the sound of a squealing 'rabbit'; as will a fox. Helen Evetts, writing in *Country Fair* magazine the early 1950s, tells us that: 'Red deer hinds and Roe deer does will come to a noise produced by blowing on the edge of an elastic band, stretched between a short length of split nut stick, grooved slightly to allow the rubber band to vibrate.'

Evetts does, however, go on to warn that: 'Neither hinds or does are interested after the young are three months old' and also mentions an occasion when she copied the roar of a Red stag by cupping her hands in front of her mouth. 'The result was alarming; the stag charged down the steep wooded face of the coombe, crossed the water just below and stood quite close to me. His eyes looked like red-hot half-crowns ...'

HARE TODAY

Brown hares are one of my favourite mammals; partly because they play a major role in many of the myths and mysteries associated with the British countryside, and partly because they are just such a beautiful creature. Hares have been around for so long and are so strongly linked with Celtic fertility rites and witches turning themselves into hares at the drop of a (pointed) hat that it's easy to think they've been in Britain forever. In actual fact, it's only the mountain hare that is native to Britain; the brown hare being introduced by the Romans less than 2,000 years ago.

Famous for the expression 'as mad as a March hare', their antics can, however, be seen at other points of the country calendar. For many years it was thought that the 'boxing' was carried out by rival males in pursuit of a female but in actual fact it is more likely that it occurs when a female is not quite ready to mate and is fending off the male's unwanted attention.

Some of the hare's activities are, though, perhaps not quite so easily and definitely explained. There are, for instance, occasional reports of 'assemblies'

Hare today...

of hares (sometimes called a 'parliament') made up of as many as forty individuals. One theory is that it's created by a number of males showing off to the ladies but, as far as I'm aware, the reasoning behind this rarely seen phenomenon has never been totally established.

For many years there was a theory that hares chewed the cud in the same manner that cows regurgitate all that they have eaten and chew it thoroughly before swallowing it again, but it is only in more recent decades that it has been discovered that the first time the food is eaten by hares it is only partially digested, compressed and softened. Refection, first noticed in rabbits, is a regular habit of the hare but, unlike cattle, partially digested food is passed through the body before being eaten again. The droppings that are refected differ in appearance from those that are finally discarded.

Naturalists will sometimes tell you that they've never seen a hare drinking and that they gain all the liquid they need from the moist vegetation they eat. Not so — and I have on at least two occasions witnessed hares drinking at the edge of a stretch of water. I have, though, never seen a witch transmogrify into a hare but, just on the off-chance that I might, I shall keep a silver bullet about my person as, according to legend, it's the only thing liable to bring down a witch when in hare form!

No sex please, we're hares

Some ancient writers believed that not only were the sexes interchangeable in hares — Sir Thomas Browne, writing *Inquiries into Common and Vulgar Errors*, said that, from Greek times on, many believed that the buck was capable, on occasions, of giving birth to young — but also that the leverets were formed in separate wombs. Claudius Aelianus, writing in the third century, claimed also that the hare 'carried some of its young half-formed in its womb, some it is in the process of bearing, others it has already borne'. Although such a procedure seems impossible it is now found that hares are unique in being able to conceive a second time even when already pregnant. Scientifically this is known as 'super-foetation'.

So, even in these days of modern research it is obvious that some areas of the hare's habits remain something of a mystery and, in certain cases, fact intermingles with fiction.

RABBIT FACTOIDS

- Rabbits are lagomorphs (from the order of *Lagomorpha*), not rodents.

- Their scientific name is *Oryctolagus cuniculus*.

- The grass and plants wild rabbits eat at dusk and dawn can be poor in nutritional value, so the rabbit will eat its own faeces in order to obtain every particle of nourishment. In common with the brown hare, this is known as 'refection'.

- A rabbit can jump up to 36in (90cm) in height and up to 10ft (3m) in length.

- Rabbits can see behind them without rotating their head – but they have a blind spot directly in front of their face … remember that when you are out stalking them with an air rifle!.

- Rabbits can't vomit.

- A male rabbit is called a buck, a female is a doe and a baby is called a kit. The babies are collectively called a litter, whilst a group of adult lagomorphs is sometimes referred to as a herd.

Some interesting snippets!

◆ Red deer were used to pull coaches during the Roman Era in the festivals related to the worship of goddess Diana, the hunting goddess.

◆ Foxes are members of the dog family – and are the only type of dog capable of retracting their claws in the same way as cats. They also have vertical pupils that look more like those of cats than they do the rounded pupils of others in the dog family.

◆ Unlike dogs and foxes, badgers have five toes and very powerful, long claws, particularly on the front feet.

◆ Every adult hedgehog has around 7,000 spines covering its back and sides.

◆ It's not true that you're never more than 6ft from a rat! Studies calculate that there are fewer than 10 million brown rats in the UK. (Source: *Wildlife Extra*)

◆ Female brown trout (*Salmo trutta*) fake orgasms to encourage males to ejaculate prematurely. By doing so, they dupe their partner into thinking he has successfully mated, before she then moves on to find a genetically better male with which to do the real thing.

◆ A trout can look and focus out of both corners of each eye simultaneously, meaning that it can see in almost every direction at once – no wonder my fishing forays are rarely as successful as I'd hope!

◆ With the above in mind, thank goodness for 'Duffer's Fortnight' – that period in the year when the mass hatching of the mayfly *Ephemera danica* can trigger a feeding frenzy in trout and even the inept like myself might stand a chance of success!

SPARROWHAWKS

Observing wildlife, you quite often see surprising things. Many years ago, I had a chicken shed with pop-holes at either end. In the habit of feeding the hens indoors, sparrows and other small birds soon learnt to frequent the shed, hopping in and out through open windows and wide mesh wire-netting. On one occasion, I happened to be watching as a sparrowhawk flew across the garden, folded its wings and, in one smooth move, dived through one pop-hole and out the other — with a sparrow in its claws. My experience was not unique; as evidenced by many similar accounts in the Letters' Page of several country magazines.

In the October 2015 copy of *The Field*, one letter writer recounted that a sparrowhawk had entered and exited their kitchen (at speed) via an open window measuring '16 × 51cm high, one of four frames in a mullioned window'. A month later, November's issue contained a reply from someone explaining that they'd witnessed a sparrowhawk swoop 'through two sides of trellis approximately 11in apart (a right-angled corner); the gap was 11cm ...'

WHO SAID IT FIRST?

'The wildlife of today is not ours to dispose of as we please. We have it in trust. We must account for it to those who come after.'

For many years, the excellent publication, *Shooting Times & Country Magazine* has included the words of King George VI (1895–1952) on its banner heading each week. Wise, erudite and true — but who uttered them first?

Sometime earlier (circa 1900), American president Theodore Roosevelt is credited as saying the following:

The wildlife of today is not ours to do with what we please. The original stock was given to us in trust for the benefit of both the present and the future. We must render an accounting of this trust to those who come after us.

Fact or Fancy?

When it comes to either 'watching wildlife' (as in the previous chapter), or 'fact or fancy', the two can very easily be confused — as they can with the ensuing chapter 'strange but true'. With this and the next, folklore and scientific biological evidence merge.

TROOPING THE COLOUR

Can pheasants and partridge see colour? Both old folklore and modern science suggest they do ... with regard to the former, writer and naturalist, W. H. Hudson, had some interesting things to say ... as did the 'Letters to the Editor' page of many a country magazine, which declared that, whilst purple crocuses would be ravaged by pheasants (and songbirds), yellow ones would be left alone.

Hudson had it that coloured streamers would keep birds out of the orchard if used en masse — and that scarlet ones worked the best. More than sixty years ago, when a swallow's nest had fallen from where it had been built and was closely examined by an interested bystander, it was noted that its lining consisted, 'entirely of feathers from Rhode Island Red fowls. Yet feathers from Plymouth Rocks, Leghorns and Orringtons had been just as accessible'. Further in the same findings came the fact that a chaffinch and a sparrow (apparently kept indoors as subject for study) would ruffle their feathers and make it obvious that something was amiss whenever a scarlet tie was worn and 'as soon as the tie was removed they became easy again'.

More modern scientific research (the results of which were published in June 2011) suggested that birds can actually see colours far better than we can. At the time, Richard Prum, a professor of ornithology, ecology, and evolutionary biology at Yale University (US), was quoted as saying: 'Our clothes were pretty drab before the invention of aniline dyes, but then colour became cheap and there was an explosion in the colorful clothes we wear today ... The same type of thing seems to have happened with birds.'

Prum's words came as a result of a study published in the journal, *Behavioral Ecology*, which found that birds can 'not only can see more colours than they have in their plumage, because of additional colour cones in their retina that are sensitive to ultraviolet range, but they also see colours that are invisible to humans.' Prum then went on to point out that: 'The startling thing to realise is that although the colours of birds look so incredibly diverse and beautiful to us, we are colour-blind compared to birds.'

THE EYES HAVE IT ...

In 1910, *The Spectator* magazine published a review of Owen Jones' *A Gamekeeper's Notebook* and questioned the veracity of a very curious country theory that had been documented within the book's pages. It concerned the belief by some that the eyes of animals magnify what they see:

> ... the eyes of animals are supposed to magnify everything they see, so that a man, for instance, appears to the animal to be twice as big, and

therefore twice as terrible. But how is it that believers in this strange notion do not see that even if animals' eyes do magnify, they magnify everything in proportion — themselves and their companions and surroundings just as surely as human beings — and that therefore there can be no more terror for them in the size of a man than in the size of a fox or partridge or caterpillar?

A SENSE OF SMELL

Keepers of old would swear by their 'secret concoctions', which they added to their pheasant feed in order to try and encourage their birds not to wander … did they work? Some think they did (and still use them), others are rather more scathing, but, faced by irrefutable evidence, may have to now eat their words.

As with birds and their ability to see colour, there has been much recent research on their ability to smell — and it appears they can. Professor Tim Birkhead, writing in the British Trust for Ornithology's 2012 spring issue of *Bird Talk*, explained that:

There are several lines of evidence. The first to be discovered was anatomical. In mammals, like ourselves, the fore part of the brain holds the 'olfactory bulb'. This is a blob of tissue that miraculously transforms electrical signals, triggered by certain airborne molecules in the nose, into something we think of as smell. In some birds the olfactory bulb is relatively large, while in other species it is quite small.

Another relevant bit of anatomy is the nasal passages near the base of the beak (their technical name is 'chonchae'). Just as in ourselves, these passages comprise delicate scrolls of tissue-covered bone … The more complex the scrolling, the greater the surface area for smell detection.

Of particular interest to those of us involved in game shooting is the fact that woodcock can smell its food through the soil and when it's observed probing away at suitable friable soil with its beak, it is not doing so randomly. Renowned traveller William Bowles, visiting Spain in the 1700s, apparently watched a

Keepers of old would swear by their 'secret concoctions'

woodcock foraging in the royal aviaries and observed that the bird appeared to be able to smell the worm before it stuck its beak into the ground. George Montagu, a British ornithologist and author of the first *Ornithological Dictionary* (1802), also commented on their remarkable ability to smell food.

Mallard drakes use their nostrils to detect pheromones released by the female a few weeks before she is due to lay and, less specifically, but fascinating nevertheless, is the relatively recent discovery that some bird species (the starling being one), deliberately place the green leaves of certain aromatic plants in their nests seemingly, it appears, to keep parasites such as lice at bay.

NB: As to how common blowflies manage to find newly shot grouse and game so quickly, experiments fifty years ago seemed to indicate that this insect has the ability to both smell and taste with its feet — now *that's* a clever trick!

GOING WITH A BANG

Having dealt with sight and smell, all that's left of the game birds' senses to discuss is that of hearing. Over the years, it has often been reported that, during World War One when the big guns were going off over the Channel in France and Belgium, cock pheasants in the south of England could hear the 'boom' and would apparently issue forth their warning cry.

Writing his regular 'Country Diary' for the *Manchester Guardian* in February 1915, the unknown diarist had this to say:

It has been suggested that unusual activity among pheasants noted on the day of the recent North Sea battle was due to their consciousness of the firing. Before we condemn as a mere fable or credulously accept the suggestion let us consider and weigh the evidence. First the Rector of Saxby, in Lincolnshire, in a letter to the 'Times', quotes his parish clerk — 'The pheasants is all over the place with their fuss.' Another observer in

Lowther, Penrith, has affirmed that the gamekeepers noticed the unusual crowing of the pheasants at the time the battle was taking place ...

Apparently the idea is that the pheasants heard the heavy firing and were disturbed. Every gamekeeper, and indeed every field ornithologist, knows that thunder invariably excites cock pheasants and causes them to crow, but this interesting fact is, as usual, omitted from most accounts of the bird, greater attention being paid to questions of rearing, slaying, and, not infrequently, cooking it ...

In my notebooks I have many references to pheasants crowing during thunderstorms, and in my 'Country Diary' for May 20, 1911, I mentioned an incident that occurred when I was cycling in Norfolk. 'I was cycling towards the coast, and when two miles away a heavy boom set the pheasants crowing in the spinneys. When I reached Palling I found the coastguards were blowing up a wreck which was a danger to the incoming fishing boats. Pheasants crowed after each explosion when, after I had left the beach, I was two or three miles away from the place.' But two or three miles is very different from one to two hundred. Suppose that the birds at Saxby were 100 miles from the spot where the battle began – they were probably much more, – what about those in Cumberland? The report of heavy guns is carried a long way, but it is a tall order to ask anyone to believe that they could be heard at two or three hundred miles. Yet on the morning of January 24 the pheasants of Saxby and Lowther Park were not the only ones which were crowing lustily.

On that morning I was in the woods near Rostherne, in Cheshire, and was so much struck by the unusual concert of excited pheasants that I made special mention of it in my notebook, though did not for one moment think of connecting it with distant battles ... in my 'Diary' for January 25, I attributed the unusual activity to vernal influences, although pheasants do not call noticeably from this reason until late February or March. If the Lowther pheasants could be moved by the uproar of battle in the North Sea, ours in Cheshire might also be affected,

Can you tell the age of a cock pheasant by the length of its spurs?

Hugh B. C. Pollard, author of *Game Birds and Game Bird Shooting* amongst other titles, reckoned that: 'Old cock pheasants with prodigious spurs may be six or even seven years old,' but that he knew 'of no really authentic and precise records'. He did, though, mention hearsay and that, occasionally: 'An oddly marked or recognisable bird is alleged to have been about "all of ten to fifteen years."'

Leg rings or wing-tags are sometimes fitted to pheasant poults immediately prior to release and if numbered or colour-coded, it is possible to tell their age accurately. Doing so can, however, cause the keeper much despondency when reports of his birds being shot on neighbouring estates begin coming in!

Goosey-goosey gander

As to the ages of geese rather than game birds, whilst it was, it must be admitted, a domestic bird rather than one found on the foreshore or wetlands, in Co. Sligo, Ireland, in 1958, a gander was recorded as being thirty-three years old. Its owner, a Mr George Huggard, apparently received it as a present when it was a young gosling and, despite its age, it was said to have been 'in perfect health, and its feathers still good and strong'.

No need for a Stannah stairlift for that particular 'goosey-goosey gander' as he wandered upstairs and downstairs ... and in his lady's chamber!

A gander was recorded as being 33 years old

for the raiders would be somewhere about an equal distance from the two counties. In spite of all our boasted knowledge we really know very little about the power of hearing in birds, and practically nothing about the sensations set up in those complicated 'semi-circular canals' which appear to regulate the equilibrium of the flying bird rather than its sense of hearing. Nevertheless we are aware that aerial vibrations that convey nothing which human ears can appreciate are set in motion by explosions; possibly the pheasants could not hear as we understand hearing, but could feel the sound waves.

If anyone has ever watched pheasants legging it down a hedgerow from cover about to be driven late in the season, they will know that their hearing is very definitely well attuned! Nonetheless, scientifically, biologists have paid relatively little attention to this particular sense – not because it is unimportant (just the opposite, given that so many birds communicate by sounds) – but because it is difficult to study.

FLIGHTS OF FANCY

Does the grouse fly faster than a partridge – or is it just an optical illusion? The renowned naturalist, wildfowler, proficient game-shot and writer, Denys Watkins-Pitchford (better known to many by his nom-de-plume of 'B B'), was of the opinion that, although 'the grouse flies faster than the partridge, due to its weight and larger wing span it is easier to see, not only because its plumage is much darker ..., but [also] because one's first shot is usually taken as the birds top the rim of the hill ...[whereas] In partridge driving, your normal position will be behind a hedge ... and often there is a distant background of trees to further confuse the eye.'

As far as it's been possible to ascertain, it seems that modern research backs up James Wentworth-Day's observations and that the red grouse does indeed fly faster than a partridge — twice as fast in fact — with the wind behind it, coming at full pelt across the moor, a grouse can reach speeds of up to 70mph; partridge, roughly half that. Figures given for pheasants seem to vary tremendously — and are given as being anywhere 'between 38–48mph ... but up to 60mph'.

Ducking the issue

Back in 1976, American John Linsenmeyer wrote a letter to a sporting magazine in which he stated that, 'as an enthusiastic wildfowler', he had read and listened to many debates as to the speed at which 'ducks routinely fly'. He then went on to cite an instance when, as he drove north on the Henry Hudson Parkway — which runs parallel to the shore of the Hudson River — he found it possible to pace three mallard flying northwards along the river for more than a mile:

Does the grouse fly faster than a partridge?

There was a light westerly breeze, blowing at four to six miles per hour roughly cross-wise to their flight. For over a mile, I kept exactly even with the three mallards whilst my speedometer read a steady 51 miles per hour.

Linsenmeyer then went on to note that: 'This may, in retrospect, explain a number of shots missed well behind'! More recent technical and scientific data seems to verify the comments and observations of Mr Linsenmeyer (when it comes to duck speed, rather than an excuse as to why we all miss on occasion!). The website for *Ducks Unlimited* (www.ducks.org) — '*banding together for waterfowl*' — cites the following:

> Most waterfowl fly at speeds of 40 to 60mph, with many species averaging roughly 50mph. With a 50mph tail wind, migrating mallards are capable of traveling 800 miles during an eight-hour flight. Studies of duck energetics show that a mallard needs to feed and rest for three to seven days to replenish the energy expended during this eight-hour journey.

The site then records this interesting fact — which, owing to my love of pure quirkiness, I couldn't possibly omit from these pages: 'The fastest duck ever recorded was a red-breasted merganser that attained a top airspeed of 100mph while being pursued by an airplane.'

FEEL THE WEIGHT OF THIS ONE!

Which of us has not been caught out as a youngster by an old hand saying; 'Cor ... this is a heavy bird ... feel the weight of it' — the idea being to get the young tyro to carry it for him! Some pheasants are, however, undoubtedly heavier than others — and much depends on the availability of feed and on the weather conditions.

Reared pheasants released on to a shoot rich in natural foodstuffs from woodland and game crops will, with the feed supplied by the keeper, obviously not be as badly affected by adverse weather conditions but, even so, they might lose weight as the natural feed decreases after Christmas. This might not be a bad thing as a loss of a certain amount of surplus fat could produce faster-flying pheasants – and perhaps that's one of the reasons that January's birds are thought better sport by many?

Generally though, a harsh January can stop fat production, and cause existing fat and muscle tissue to be used for warmth ... with a corresponding weight loss. Even with normal January weather, game birds may stop producing fat and use what they eat for warmth without using existing fat or muscle but, if particularly mild conditions occur in the New Year, a part of their diet can continue to be used to make body fat and increase weight.

NB: No matter what the weather, it's important to carry on feeding hand-reared birds long after the shooting season has ended, and certainly into the spring months when natural feed in the shape of new vegetation, seeds and insects begin to show once more.

In league with the Devil

Sometimes those who should know better fail to check their facts – or perhaps they keep things fanciful because it suits their cause better.

The League Against Cruel Sports (LACS), for example, lay claim to some rather spurious 'facts' in their propaganda. They have, in the past few years, claimed amongst other things, that 200 animals an hour are killed in UK snares set for foxes – when you multiply that figure up into a daily, weekly, monthly and annual rate, that's a lot of animals falling foul to snares – if that is, their 'facts' were true. Likewise, in separate publicity, a phenomenal number of badgers are supposed to be accidentally (and illegally) caught in snares: in actual fact, the figure the LACS claim are caught is actually around the estimated total badger population – why then do we see so many in the countryside (and as roadkill)?

Strange But True

Sometimes, as was discussed at the beginning of the last chapter, it's difficult to differentiate between 'fact or fancy' and 'strange but true'. When it comes to the subject of poaching, for instance, children's author, Roald Dahl has a lot to answer for as a result of his 1975 book, *Danny, the Champion of the World*! Readers of the book (and viewers of the film made as a result) might easily be left wondering whether it's possible to poach pheasants in the way Dahl describes Danny doing— seemingly it is!

The Close Season and Poaching

'The greatest division of the year is February 2nd, if we may take that as the most typical date for the beginning of the ... close season, when it is against the law to kill game ... The increasing army of poachers ... pay little attention to the date. A man found last year shooting pheasants on the nest ... excused himself by saying "But, look you, they are then easiest to kill". The prime evil of poaching is its cruelty. Fish-hooks baited with raisins were recently found in one of the Home Counties.
It would be to the good if the penalties for poaching, whatever they are, were very greatly increased if the game were killed in the close season, or by any such cruelty as the fish-hook or steel trap inflicts.'

The Spectator, February 1927

FISHING FOR THE TRUTH!

Fish-hooks tied to fishing line and baited with raisins feature in both *Danny, the Champion of the World* and in the *Spectator* report of 1927. The method might seem fanciful but it's true. So too is the even stranger idea of catching pheasants with the aid of a conical-shaped piece of paper or, as described by George Herter, in *Herter's Professional Guide's Manual Vol II*, a piece of tree bark.

> Take a piece of tree bark such as birch bark or the smooth inner bark of most any tree. Make a cone from it like an ice cream cone or a little larger. Hold the cone together with a piece of twig, wood or vine. Smear fresh sticky tree resin on the inside of the cone. Fill the end of the cone with the seeds or grain that the birds you desire feed on. Lay a trail of seeds or grain up to the cone. Place the cone in a place the birds frequent. Pheasant, grouse, partridge, or quail will feed on the trail of seeds or grain up to the cone and then will reach for the seeds in the end of the cone. The sticky resin will stick to their head feathers and hold the cone on to their head. They will not struggle but will just sit and not move at all. You can walk right up to them and kill them.
>
> This cone trick of getting game birds originated in England. Poachers have used it for centuries. Today they make the cones from paper and glue a one inch strip of fly paper inside of the cone to stick on the bird's head feathers. A good poacher in two weeks' time can get every game bird in the area he puts his cones out in.

As to the fish-hook and raisin method so beloved of Danny – and now described online (no pun intended!):

> '... an old poaching trick was to put down food for a few days, get them used to feeding, then thread a raisin on a fish-hook attached to a length of cotton or fishing line. The birds take the raisin and, in doing so, the

hook sticks in their mouth or down their throat ... you can then walk up to them and pick them up.

Farm gate 'freebie'

With the price of game so low one would have thought the problem of poaching would be much reduced. Apropos to which, I seem to recall the story of a farmer who, having some of his pheasants shot from the roadsides, tried a novel solution. At the farm entrance he put up a notice: 'Please do not poach my pheasants – call at the house for a free one!' Unfortunately, history fails to record how many, if any, availed themselves of the offer.

GANGLAND KILLERS

"Do you mean to tell me," shouted the Rat, thumping with his little fist upon the table, "that you've heard nothing about the Stoats and Weasels?"

"What, the Wild Wooders?" cried Toad, trembling in every limb. "No, not a word! What have they been doing?"

Conversation in Kenneth Grahame's famous book, *The Wind in the Willows*, makes mention of the fear and awe in which weasels and stoats – but especially stoats – were held by the other creatures inhabiting its pages. Long thought to hunt in packs, there have been plenty of accounts written by quite respected countrymen of them doing so. Amongst them comes this one written by J. C. Atkinson in January, 1844:

It has come to my knowledge that the stoat not only hunts by scent but also in packs and in full cry ... a gentleman of Hutton was fishing one day in the Whitadder when his attention was aroused ... presently emerged from the covert, a pack of stoats 'just' added he, 'as you might see a pack of hounds come into sight, first one or two, perhaps, and close behind, there or four others and so on.' The stoats were seven in number and stuck to the trail in gallant style.

There have been many other such similar sightings, some of which are far more recent. It is, however, now accepted that they are most likely to be just a family group rather than any gathering more sinister. Stoat bitches can give birth to as many as thirteen youngsters in a litter and each of these are mature enough to hunt with their mother within a very short space of time – and can hunt and kill for themselves by the age of around twelve weeks.

Like many other animals, the female is capable of delayed implantation* but far more unusual is the fact that the male stoat will mate with both their unweaned offspring and their mother, thus ensuring the best chances of survival – and the likelihood of a casual observer seeing what he or she might suppose to be a marauding pack.

In delayed implantation the embryo does not immediately implant in the uterus, but it is maintained in a state or dormancy. No development takes place during this period and as a result the normal gestation period is extended, sometimes by as much a one year, depending on the animal species under discussion.

— COUNTING CROWS —

There's many an account as to the astuteness of members of the corvid family – and just as many suggestions given as how to overcome the problem should you ever be wanting to shoot a crow, magpie or jay at their nest as they sit on eggs in the spring.

Most will tell you that, whilst crows and their ilk cannot count, they are aware of someone setting up hide near their nest, so the best way to ensure getting a shot as one or other of the parent birds come into the vicinity is to take a friend with you to the hiding place. After a few minutes, the friend should leave and, in theory at least, the wary, wily birds will be lulled into a false sense of security and continue their normal activities — leaving themselves at the mercy of you and your gun tucked away in the hide.

Scientists beg to differ and will tell you that, whilst most birds can make calculations by discriminating between groups of dots, the crow's brain simply ignores the arrangement of dots and instead, like humans, can actually count due to individual nerve cells in its brain.

Helen Ditz and Professor Andreas Nieder of the University of Tübingen, Germany, have recently come to the conclusion that crows 'have a reasoning ability of a human seven-year-old' and that their brain nerve cells, or neurons, 'ignore the dot size, shape and arrangement and only extract their number'. So that's another traditional countryman's ruse spoilt by scientific research!

A PARTRIDGE IN A KETTLE

Sometimes truth is very definitely stranger than fiction – as this entry in the *Haverhill Echo* dated 31 December 1904 can testify:

The following story is culled from the *Weekly Telegraph* which tells the story of a retriever dog. Some years ago this incident occurred at Long Melford, the shooter was standing under a fence when he saw a French partridge fly straight to a fence, he was about to fire when the bird dropped into a ditch opposite where he was standing, he immediately sent the dog after it about a hundred yards away, it returned with some feathers in its mouth, He sent it in again telling the dog to fetch, it returned carrying an old kettle minus its handle with the partridge peeping out. No doubt the bird ran into the kettle to escape but owing to its small aperture the dog was unable to get the bird out, the dog thinking it best to bring the lot rather than disappoint its master. This was witnessed by several gentlemen in the party and the bird was in no way injured.

Some grey partridge factoids

◆ Although much research into wild partridge management is recent, work studying their ecology actually began in the early 1930s.

◆ Grey partridges pair up during February to breed and will do so during their first year.

◆ Spring dispersal of grey partridge pairs happens over short distances. Many partridge pairs spend their entire lives in the same three or four fields.

◆ For the two to three weeks after hatching, more than 90 per cent of a grey partridge chick's diet needs to be protein-rich insects and other invertebrates, not seeds.

HOW PARTRIDGES PAIR — AND WHY PHEASANTS FLIRT

Pheasants begin courtship by dropping one wing and dancing round the hen in a circle … if receptive, she will crouch in submission, dip her head and spread her wings to the side for balance. Some of the more aggressive pheasant cocks will not only 'dance' round the hen bird in a circle, but they will also raise their hackles and drop and extend both wings and puff out all their body feathers to give their admiring harem (and other males) the impression of greater size.

Both pheasant and partridge mate by the male dipping his tail to the side of the hens until their cloacal meet — the 'cloacal kiss'. Since the male's mating organ is located inside him on the middle and front portion of his cloaca, his must touch that of the hen in order to transfer sperm. The male then hops off, the hen shakes out her feathers — and both go about their business as if nothing has happened!

SEVEN WHISTLERS

Any wildfowlers will recognise the noise of whistling wigeon as they come in last thing at night or before dawn in the morning. Their calls (and those of some other wildfowl) can sound quite unearthly and, in the past, has resulted in our ancestors building certain superstitions around them. Writing in *Birds in Legend, Fable and Folklore* (1923), Ernest Ingersoll recalled 'the queer British superstition of the Seven Whistlers' and quotes Wordsworth as saying of 'his ancient Dalesman':

He the seven birds hath seen that never part,
Seen the Seven Whistlers on their nightly rounds
And counted them.

Ingersoll then goes on to say:

> The idea that the wailing of invisible birds is a warning of danger direct from Providence prevails especially in the English colliery districts, where wildfowl, migrating at night and calling to one another as they go, supply exactly the right suggestion to the timid. Sailors fear them as 'storm-bringers'. Even more horrifying is the primitive Welsh conception (probably capable of a similar explanation) of the Three Birds of Rhiannon, wife of Pwyll, ruler of Hades, who could sing the dead to life and the living into the sleep of death. Luckily they were heard only at the death of great heroes in battle.

'HERE KITTY, KITTY!'

A stuffed cat is a deadly lure when it comes to vermin control (but a model owl or similar might be a more acceptable alternative in this day and age!) Back in the day, however – in 1938, to be precise – when Gilbertson & Page published their booklet, *The Control of Vermin*, it was advised that:

> The sportsman or trapper, should place himself by a tree trunk and in perfect stillness watch for birds flitting in … the best method is to use a stuffed cat as lure. Don't throw away every dead cat; skin it, put a little alum on the inside of the skin and let it dry for a couple of days. Stuff the skin with hay, and, with pieces of wire as props for legs and tail, and glass beads for eyes, make the best representation of a live cat possible.

Cat-calling

In his book, *The Autobiography of an English Gamekeeper* (1892), John Wilkins went one step further in describing how best to use a dead cat as a lure to attract winged predators:

Take a dead cat, and put it into a magpie's nest when the bird is absent, then make an arbour, close by, to hide yourself in, which you will have plenty of time to do before the bird comes back to her nest to sit. When she returns she spies her enemy the cat, coiled up in her nest fast asleep, as she supposes, and she immediately begins to call out and abuse the cat. She makes such a noise that she soon brings up other flying vermin from the adjoining woods. Don't shoot the mother magpie at first; let her have plenty of time to abuse the cat, and swear at it for being in her nest, thus attracting all her neighbours. These latter, on seeing what's up, perch themselves over the nest and join in a chorus screaming out to awaken the cat and make her quit. Now's your time, when you see a good chance to kill four or five birds together, let fly into the middle of the lot. Down they come at the foot of the tree, and don't now show yourself, but slip another charge into the gun, for the rest will not leave if they don't see you. Very soon they will come and have another try to wake up the cat, and so you can get another shot, and kill two or three more.

Kitty killers

That cats, particularly feral ones, are 'lethal weapons of destruction' on both the shoot and in a domestic situation, there can be no doubt. Recent statistics have it that: 'In the UK alone, domestic cats kill 57 million mammals a year, 27 million birds and 5 million reptiles and amphibians.'

Be that as it may, there are many who think that a home and domesticity is incomplete without a cat about the place.

Sporting Domesticity

Despite what some people think, to those of us involved in field sports, the killing of an animal, bird or fish for the table is but a small part of the day. Far more important is the camaraderie of friends, the enjoyment of a certain place and, at the end of it all, the chance to reflect back on the day's sport – preferably with a drink to hand whilst sitting by a blazing log fire!

A KNOTTY PROBLEM

There are few things more welcoming than a blazing log fire in the hearth of a shooting lodge – the problem is deciding what wood burns best. *The Firewood Poem* should help:

Beechwood fires are bright and clear
If the logs are kept a year,
Chestnut's only good they say,
If for logs 'tis laid away.
Make a fire of Elder tree,
Death within your house will be;
But ash new or ash old,
Is fit for a queen with crown of gold

Birch and fir logs burn too fast
Blaze up bright and do not last,
it is by the Irish said
Hawthorn bakes the sweetest bread.
Elm wood burns like churchyard mould,
E'en the very flames are cold
But ash green or ash brown
Is fit for a queen with golden crown

Poplar gives a bitter smoke,
Fills your eyes and makes you choke,
Apple wood will scent your room
Pear wood smells like flowers in bloom
Oaken logs, if dry and old
keep away the winter's cold
But ash wet or ash dry
a king shall warm his slippers by

There are several variations to this poem but this is reckoned to be the original, written by Celia Congreve, and was first published in *The Times* newspaper in March 1930 ... unless you know differently!

Salty solutions

According to *The Field Book of Country Queries* (1989), you can prevent coniferous wood from sparking on the lodge fire in the following way:

> These woods contain small knots ... which 'pop' under heat. The simplest way to check the sparking is to sprinkle salt lightly on the logs when they have begun to burn and repeat when fresh logs are added. It helps if the logs are cut in small, chunky pieces and are added with the bark facing inwards. Feed a fire from the back, placing fresh logs more or less behind those already burning.

Fire, beer and cider

John Udal, in his work, *Dorsetshire Folklore* (1922), noted that:

> It was customary in many farmhouses on Christmas Eve for a large block of wood to be brought into the kitchen, and an immense fire having been made up, the farm labourers would come around and sit around it, or as many as were able would crowd into the chimney corner, and drink beer and cider. This was what was usually called the Christmas brown.

I have to admit that his description sounds pretty much like an average group of beaters to me!

BIG BREAKFAST

As we all know, a good breakfast is essential before a day's shooting but what actually constitutes a 'good' breakfast? Much as we'd all like to hope that it includes a 'full English' of sausage and bacon, together with copious amounts of toast slathered with lashings of butter, I fear it may not – or does it?

Nutritional advice is notoriously fickle: fat makes you fat; fat makes you thin; carbs are bad; carbs are good ... and so on and so forth.

Recent research has it that there's no conclusive evidence either way; however, the idea that a hearty breakfast is the most important meal of the day is nowadays widely assumed — and seemingly all as a result of advertising from as far back as the 1920s.

During that time, America's public relations guru Edward Bernays was tasked with increasing bacon consumption and (despite the fact that, at the time, Americans generally favoured a light breakfast), he reckoned that a good way to do so would be to persuade them to eat bacon as part of their first meal of the day. With that in mind, Bernays asked doctors to confirm that 'a hearty breakfast was better than a light breakfast to replace the energy lost by the body at night' — and a staggering 4,500 of them did so. As a result of which, Bernays reported the doctors' 'findings' in the press — and had bacon adverts strategically placed alongside the headlines.

TAKE SOME WATER WITH IT!

It's not unusual to walk into the shooting lodge and be faced by fellow Guns with a glass of water in an attempt to rehydrate themselves after wine and a good dinner the evening before. There are even some shoots that, as a matter of course, provide small bottles of water for the Guns to take with them whilst out on the shoot.

Many will quote the importance of drinking 'eight glasses of water a day', which, as the research says; 'is great if you enjoy urinating, but generally it's unnecessary'. Bottled water companies have helped reinforce existing hydration misinformation through exaggerated health marketing, and we lap it up. Consumption of bottled water has shot up — in the UK, it's now 100 times higher than in 1980.

Take some water with it!

WHAT'S YOUR POISON?

No shooting day can be considered complete without a drink — but should it be alcohol or tea? In the early 1800s, the third Marchioness of Bath, writing in her book, *Domestic Economy*, decried tea because, 'besides being good for nothing [it] has badness in it ...' She then went on to prove that, whereas, tea-drinking would cost £10 a year on average 'and do them nothing but harm', home-brewed beer would cost but £7.5s and opined that it would 'benefit them in every way'. It would appear that there's a very definite case for sloe gin!

TEATIME

After a day's shooting, there's always time for tea, cake and biscuits before then perhaps going on to a G & T before supper. If you are a fan of dunking biscuits — and let's face it, who isn't? — it might help to know the findings of some recent research.

Seemingly, Dr Stuart Farrimond, in conducting experiments for *Guro* magazine, discovered that a Rich Tea is the best one to choose as they can hold it together for up to twenty seconds. Hobnobs were the worst and disintegrated in only four seconds. 'The larger oat particles provide less structural strength to the biscuit,' explained Dr Farrimond. Not only that, but his team (yes, there were more than just Dr Farrimond conducting this research) reckoned that your tea should be allowed to cool for three minutes in order to give your biscuit the best chance of survival.

Cream tea etiquette!

Better than biscuits, sometimes you may be fortunate enough to be offered a full-blown cream tea experience, in which case, it might be useful to include here some of the facts and fabrications of cream tea etiquette!

Pour in the tea first, followed by milk ... the fad of putting the milk in first began in the days of fine bone china when to pour in hot tea first ran the risk of cracking one of your host's best tea cups.

Contrary to popular opinion, sticking your little finger out, does not a gentleman make! Always hold the cup between your thumb and forefinger.

You shouldn't need to use a knife to cut your scone – a perfectly baked one will just break apart with a gentle, quick twist – just make sure there's a plate to hand to catch the crumbs ... although, on a shoot day, there's quite likely to be a dog around to hoover up any crumbs that do end up on the floor!

Spoon then spread. Spoon the required amount of jam and cream on to your plate first – and then spread them on the scone with your knife.

Jam before cream, or cream before jam? The jury is still out on this. Although there are regional differences in thinking, Debrett's – that font of all society knowledge – says that the jam should always go on before the cream ... and you should never use the whipped variety: it's just not done, you know!

PASS THE SMELLING SALTS

What a lot of nonsense has been written in the past about women in the field. At one time, a woman's place was considered to be in the home (an opinion held mainly by men, of course!) and any active participation in game shooting was considered not to be quite correct. Seemingly it was okay for ladies to ride to hounds, but to get up close and personal with a shotgun or rifle was likely to upset their 'feminine sensibilities' due to the likelihood of blood and guts being seen at close hand.

It was even said that a woman out partridge shooting, for example, was likely to deter rather than attract 'serious suitors' and – shock, horror – put their prospects of matrimony and domesticity at risk. If, despite a man's best efforts, a lady couldn't be dissuaded from game shooting, it was recommended that she should learn to dispatch wounded game without 'shuddering about it'.

However, at least according to Boria Majumdar and Fan Hong, editors of *Modern Sport – The Global Obsession* (Routledge); 'Sporting women often confronted head-on the myth of "tender" female sensibilities and made it quite clear that the emotional distress caused by hunting, shooting and fishing could be handled by women as well as men.'

ANNIE GET YOUR GUN

Annie Oakley was very definitely a pioneer of sexual equality when it came to shooting! Even as a child she was so skilled with a gun that she almost single-handedly supported her mother and siblings by shooting and selling game to local shops and restaurants. In fact, so successful was she that she was able to repay the entire mortgage on the family farm.

Entering a shooting contest in 1875, she beat the renowned marksman Frank E. Butler – whom she later married. The couple began a touring demonstration of their shooting skills and Annie adopted the stage name

Watanya Cicilla. It was, though, only after joining up with Buffalo Bill and his Wild West Show in 1885 that Annie became really famous and, together with Frank, travelled all across America and Europe. As well as European royalty, she also befriended Sitting Bull, who symbolically adopted her and named her Little Sure Shot.

WHAT'S IN A NAME?

Some people seem to have surnames particularly appropriate to their chosen occupation or sporting interest. Quite often these did, of course, originate as a result of the professions of long ago; the surname 'Fletcher' would, for instance, indicate an ancient ancestor's connection with the bow and arrow weaponry trade of centuries ago. Others may be a little more obvious – and certainly appropriate for a book of this nature!

Should your surname happen to be either 'Pheasant' or 'Partridge', you'll probably know its origins already; however, for those who don't, here it is – at least according to the Oxford University Press *Dictionary of Family Names*:

Pheasant – English (Wolverhampton): metonymic occupational name for a breeder of pheasants or a birdcatcher, or a nickname for someone thought to resemble the bird, from Middle English *fesaunt* ...

Partridge – English: from Middle English pertriche ... (via Old French and Latin from Greek *perdix*), either a metonymic occupational name for a hunter of the bird or a nickname for someone with some fancied resemblance to it, or a habitational name for someone living at a house distinguished by the sign of a partridge. This surname has been established in Ireland since the seventeenth century.

Interestingly, the 1891 England and Wales Census Data showed that the majority of people with 'Pheasant' as a surname lived in north-east England, whilst most people with the surname 'Partridge' lived in the Midlands ... make of that what you will.

LAVISH YOUR LEATHER

Over the centuries there have been many ideas and myths regarding the best way to clean leather, particularly leather boots. Beau Brummel, the Regency 'dandy', was supposed to have insisted that his hunting boots were cleaned with champagne and would, on occasion, clean a town boot himself just to show a servant how it should be done. This apparently even extended to blacking the soles!

Many shooting men of the past would have had no idea how to care for their leather goods, there always being someone else on hand to do it for them. In this day and age, however, few of us are in the privileged position of employing a 'Jeeves' and it's necessary to see to such things oneself.

Always remove dirt and mud from cartridge bags, gun slips, boots and shoes, and if they are wet, place them to dry out naturally in a warm airy place – but not right on top of a stove or radiator. Special bags of crystals that absorb moisture can be bought to put inside boots or Wellingtons and these help to wick away the dampness from inside the boots. These bags must then be dried out before using them again. Failing that, the old traditional standby of using scrunched up newspapers stuffed inside boots certainly helps in absorbing wet resulting from walking through an over-deep puddle or stretch of water.

Cleaning leather

Years ago, it was accepted practice to treat leather, including outdoor boots, with a good application of dubbin; allowing it to soak in and then finishing off with polish or cream. Nowadays, all my leather boots, and indeed, normal day-to-day shoes, are kept in fine form by the occasional application of the natural but almost magical Renapur Leather Balsam. It does, quite literally, what it says on the tin in that it 'protects, waterproofs and nourishes all leathers, restoring their original softness and colour, preserving its looks and so extending its life'.

There are, of course, many other products that keep leather in good repair, but remember that some that are silicone-based and, whilst helping to make items waterproof, will not necessarily 'feed' the leather in any way.

HAUNTED HOUSES AND GHOSTLY GAMEKEEPERS

Many a shooting lodge, hunting box and fishing hut is said to be haunted — perhaps unsurprising given the isolation and often gloomy, daunting appearance of many. As David S. D. Jones and I noted in our book, *Sporting Lodges: Sanctuaries, Havens and Retreats* (Quiller, 2013), Scotland has more than its fair share. There is, for instance, at Edinbane on the Isle of Skye, 'The Lodge' which used to be a sixteenth century hunting lodge (and is now a hotel), in the grounds of which were, at some time, hanged criminals whose spirits are said to still remain. At Glamis Castle, best known as being the home of the late Elizabeth, The Queen Mother, but which was originally built in the thirteenth century as a hunting lodge for the Scottish Crown, apparently walk the ghosts of the 'Grey Lady' and the 2nd Lord Glamis, Earl Beardie.

In Ireland, near Dublin, at Killakee House, built in 1765 as a hunting lodge for the Conolly family, there has supposedly been seen black cats, blue nuns and an Indian man, while in England, at a pub that stands on the site of Manor Lodge, Sheffield (the sporting residence of various Earls of Shrewsbury), occasionally appears the apparition of a figure — thought by some to be a prisoner of state once housed at the Lodge. At The Dering Arms, Kent, is sometimes seen an old lady in a bonnet. This particular pub, situated in Pluckley — said to be the most haunted village in England — was originally another old hunting lodge but who the old lady was or the significance of her appearance was not really made clear in any records.

Ghostly gamekeepers

Another lady, this time wearing a red riding habit, is reputed to ride towards Gwrych Castle at Llanddulas in Wales, and is reckoned to be a previous owner killed in an accident on the hunting field: why she should be wearing red is open to speculation as it is not a colour that ladies would ever have worn whilst out following hounds. Also in Wales, at Denbigh Moors, there are the ruins of a hunting lodge called 'Plas Pren'— around which is said to have been observed a moving skeleton with glowing bones!

Phantom poacher turned ghostly gamekeeper

I once worked for a head keeper who I swear was supernatural in the way that, no matter where I was or what I was doing on the shoot, he seemed to know my exact whereabouts and would often materialise behind me like a phantom. Usually when I was doing something I shouldn't, or taking a short cut in order to get a job done!

There are, though, a surprising number of 'real' ghostly gamekeeper stories. Take, for instance, the tale of Robert Scott, a keeper at Margam Castle, Port Talbot, Wales, who was killed by poachers and whose angry ghost has been frequently seen on the castle steps.

Similarly, in 1891, at Aldbury, on the Stocks estate, Hertfordshire, three poachers were surprised by two of the estate's gamekeepers and 'a violent confrontation took place'. After a struggle both of the gamekeepers were killed — and the poachers were subsequently apprehended and sentenced to death. Afterwards it was rare for anyone to go anywhere near where the confrontation took place as it was thought the ghosts of all five men walked the area.

At Tatton Old Hall in Cheshire, whilst the building is known to be haunted by a number of female spirits, the ghost that causes most concern is male — and a poacher turned gamekeeper. Known to all as 'Tom', the apparition is variously described as being nasty, mean and drunk ... and is said to torment female visitors to the hall. Some might say that Tom reminds them of present-day keepers they have met but I couldn't possibly comment!

Dog Days

Continuing in similar vein with regard to the ghostly goings-on mentioned at the end of the last chapter, whilst the hunting world is full of tales of 'hell-hounds' and headless horsemen riding over the moors at night, it is hard to imagine similar scenarios concerning lovable Labradors and cuddly cocker spaniels. There are, though, some Guns who swear that they've felt the presence of an old, long-gone shooting companion sitting at their feet whilst in a hide waiting for pigeon or duck; thus emphasizing that obvious special bond between dog and owner.

HANDSOME IS AS HANDSOME DOES

Do we need to have a gun dog breed for gun dog purposes? Some say yes; others no. 'It's all in generations of breeding, so yes, most definitely,' frequently proclaim the traditionalists. In the 'no, it's not necessary at all' camp, I've met at least three people who have used a German Shepherd for beating and retrieving and, although it seems a contradiction bearing in mind the fact that they are more used to breaking the backs of rats (and would therefore, be

deemed to be naturally 'hard-mouthed'), many who have put a terrier to work on the shooting field.

A terrier's prowess is, it must be admitted, usually found out by accident. One keen shooting man, for example, had one who came into his own after the death of a working Labrador. '... he barely missed a day ... and became so good that I never needed to replace my Lab. His real forte was finding grouse that were hidden in long heather ... And he would guard my butt when grouse were laid out on top of it ...'

NEVER A BAD COLOUR

They say a 'good horse is never a bad colour'. The same should apply to gun dogs but seemingly it doesn't. Some cocker spaniel owners, for instance, would never entertain a 'yellow/fox-red' type believing there's something in their brain make-up that makes them less easy to train than other colours. As far as pale-coloured yellow Labradors or golden retrievers are concerned, traditionalists will often not entertain them – but only for the simple reason that they are more conspicuous in a hide.

Conversely, for a long time the majority of English springer spaniels had a great deal of liver colouring about their body but, over recent years, several strains have become whiter and whiter; particularly amongst those bred by field-triallers who reckon that a light-coloured dog is easier to see working in the undergrowth – and therefore more likely to be noticed by the judges.

Chocolate Labradors were first noted in 1892 but it wasn't until the 1930s

that they (then called 'liver') began to be seen about on the shooting field and in the show-ring — and it was the 1960s before their coat colour became known as 'chocolate'.

As to that age-old argument about 'golden' Labradors, most would agree there is no such thing and that they should be correctly referred to as 'yellow' — leaving the prefix 'golden' to the retriever.

'Temper, Temper'

Light-coloured eyes were once said to be a sign of a dog's 'treacherous temper'. Whether there's any truth in the adage is open to doubt but the subject of genetics affecting their colouration is a complicated one – and is perhaps best explained here: *www.doggenetics.co.uk/eyes.html*

Exactly what dogs can see (especially at night) is far more easily covered – as in this section from the latest digital edition of the *Merck Manual of Pet Health*:

> Dogs can see movement and light much better than people. In the retina of the eye, dogs have more of a specific type of cell called a 'rod', which is good at collecting dim light, so they have better night vision. A reflective layer in the dog's eye, called the 'tapetum lucidum', magnifies incoming light. This reflective layer lends a characteristic blue or greenish glint to dogs' eyes when light (for example, headlights of passing cars) shines into them at night.
>
> However, dogs do not have as much visual acuity as people, meaning that they cannot distinguish fine details as well. They also cannot differentiate colours as well because they have fewer of the cells in the retina called 'cones', which are responsible for colour vision. Contrary to popular belief, however, dogs are not completely colour-blind.

WHY DOES MY DOG DO *THAT*?

Just when you'd resigned yourself to the fact that the reason your dog spends ages going round in a circle or backing up to the base of a tree before performing a 'poo' is simply because they can, a study of such behaviour now tells us that free-roaming dogs choose the direction they relieve themselves based on the planet's magnetic field.

The study, published in the journal, *Frontiers in Zoology*, claims that, not only do dogs use the Earth's magnetic field when they're relieving themselves, they also do so in a particular direction. After examining seventy dogs over two years (and 1,893 defecations and 5,582 urinations – it's a tough job but apparently somebody's got to do it!), researchers found that under 'calm magnetic field conditions', dogs preferred to 'excrete with the body being aligned along the north–south axis', avoiding east–west altogether. Why they do so was unclear, according to the study but even so, the researchers and scientists involved reckon that 'the findings open "new horizons" for further research in organisms' use of magnetic fields for direction, as well as magnetic fields produced by living organisms.'

Also still unclear is whether dogs consciously align themselves in such a way: i.e. can they somehow 'sense' the magnetic field/compass direction (by sight, hearing or smell), or are their preferred actions based on the fact that they '"feel better/more comfortable or worse/less comfortable" in a certain direction.'

Too shy to s**t

And, bringing up the rear, as it were, why is it that, whilst preferably faced on a north–south axis, your dog tends to watch you as he or she prepares to poo? Some owners think it because the dog is embarrassed and is wishing you would look away or give him privacy – yes, really, they do.

In reality, it seems that it's more to do with the 'pack instinct' and risk element involved as they are at their most vulnerable when defecating. As the scientists have it: 'He must posture to perform the task and because of this, he is not in a position to readily fight or flee. In fact, it would be rather difficult for him to defend himself or to escape danger while he is eliminating. Your dog is instinctively aware of his defencelessness.' But they also know that, through domestication, they are part of a human pack now – and that you in turn, are a member of their family group: 'If your dog watches you during this time, it is because he is depending on you to give him a body language signal or "heads up" if he should be afraid. He may also be looking to you to possibly defend him should the need arise. If you suddenly leap away, you can bet your dog will respond also.'

Conversely, some dogs will not defecate with anyone watching, or whilst on a lead — I wonder what the canine behavourists make of that one?

WALKING THE DOG

According to research carried out by a dog food manufacturer, walking your dog is better than going to the gym. The findings revealed that the average owner will walk the equivalent distance of London to Bangkok during their dog's lifetime. And they will clock up 676 miles a year — the same as twenty-six marathons — 208 more than the average member of a gym.

Dog walking lowers the blood pressure and slows heart rates (although the gun dog owner might occasionally find that difficult to believe when his dog hurtles off unbidden to retrieve a bird in the middle of the drive — and in front of fellow Guns). If you want to 'power walk', the study recommended that some of the best canine companions are springer spaniels, setters and weimaraners, or, if you merely want to walk briskly, retrievers and Jack Russells.

RUB-A-DUB-DUB ...

The unknown reviewer of Owen Jones' *A Gamekeeper's Notebook* — after previously being extremely disparaging about whether or not an animal's eyes magnified to twice actual size (*see* 'THE EYES HAVE IT ...' in Chapter 10) — went on to say:

We like much better the chronicles of simple fact, particularly the quaint country recipes, such as the best kind of dog-wash, which is an armful of foxglove plants boiled in a copper and rubbed into the dog's coat before lathering him with soft soap ... 'and his coat will look fit to go to a wedd'n' after that', so a keeper of the old school informs us. We get, incidentally, a pleasant picture of the gamekeeper's wife horrified at the sight of a retriever being lathered in her new washtub, – 'a happy look comes over the dog's face', we are told, if he is cleverly rubbed and soaked.

Given that foxgloves produce 'digitalis', from which poisons can be derived; despite the 'happy look' on a dog's face as it is being bathed and massaged, it might be prudent to seek out potentially safer alternatives! Whilst shampoo intended for humans will do the job, they may not actually do your dog's coat and skin much good. Without getting too technical, an important component of human skin is what is known as the 'acid mantle', which acts as a barrier protecting the porous topmost layer of the skin from environmental contaminants such as bacteria and viruses. The acid mantle can also be defined as the relative pH balance of the skin.

The pH scale ranges from 0 to 14, with levels less than 6.4 considered high acidity, and levels more than 6.4 considered high alkalinity. The normal range of skin pH levels for humans is 5.2 to 6.2, which means it tends to be on the acidic side, and shampoos and skin products are formulated specifically to maintain this balance.

In dogs, however, depending on breed, gender and climate, the pH levels range from 5.5 to 7.5 – tending toward a more alkaline concentration. Therefore, if a shampoo that is formulated for human skin is used on a dog, the dog's acid mantle may be disrupted, thus creating an environment where bacteria, parasites, and viruses can run riot. So, just as you would look for a shampoo that helps maintain the pH balance of your own scalp, you should also only ever use a shampoo specifically intended for dogs.

SHORT BACK AND SIDES

Even a bath will not always clean up a particularly muddy spaniel – and even if it does, it's only likely to be a temporary measure until the next ditch, seed-ridden field or briar-dense hedgerow is encountered!

Some advocate stripping out the thickest of a spaniel's coat while others maintain to do so removes some of the outer 'guard hairs' considered necessary for the dog's warmth and protection. Most compromise by simply trimming the 'feathers' and ears with a pair of thinning shears but, especially when dogs are working during the early part of the season (on the grouse moors, for example), it may pay to take more drastic measures and strip the dog's coat out completely. Apart from anything else, it's easier to see any wounds that might have been sustained whilst working, and to locate and remove any ticks picked up from the bracken or similar rough cover.

ITCHY AND SCRATCHY

There's a commonly held myth that short-haired dogs cause fewer allergy problems than those with long hair. In actual fact, all dogs – short-haired, long-haired, wire-haired, wire-coated — can cause allergic reactions in some owners. Such reactions are not caused by the hair but by 'dander' (the tiny scales of dead skin) and by sebaceous and salivary gland secretions; therefore, short-haired dogs can potentially cast off just as many allergens into the immediate environment as do those with long hair.

TO KENNEL OR NOT TO KENNEL — THAT IS THE QUESTION!

Should you keep your working dog indoors as part of the family, or should it be kennelled outdoors? It is a subject that has vexed gun dog owners and trainers for many a long year. A recent survey of 23,000 dog owners, reported in the *Daily Telegraph*, revealed that more than half allowed their dogs to sleep on their beds. Quite how many of these were working gun dogs, the survey didn't divulge — but I'm willing to bet it wasn't many! Much does, of course, depend on the breed of dog and the owner's lifestyle, but there's far more to it than that.

A commonly held school of thought suggests that a dog under training is better off in a kennel environment because, when out and about with its trainer, it will be focused on its handler (on the other hand, there are also those who feel that a young dog kept within the family environment will be far better 'humanised'). A compromise might be to use a 'cage' as a kennel in the house — which will allow a dog its own secure environment to which it can go to get out of the way of family hustle and bustle. This is an option that wasn't open to keepers of the past as 'cages' are a relatively new idea.

Alternatively, consider an outdoor kennel for the times you are out of the house, but allow your dog(s) access to your home at times suitable to you. An outdoor kennel can also be useful for the times when dogs are brought in muddy and wet after a day's work — although they should, of course, always be towel-dried before being kennelled, putting them in there for an hour or so

Kennel dog ...

... Kitchen dog

will prevent much dirt from finding its way into your home.

However they are constructed, outdoor kennels must be dry and draught-proof; preferably with a raised bed both in the sleeping area and in the run. Some manufactured kennels have an option of a covered roof over the outdoor run; they will obviously cost more but are undoubtedly worth considering. Most importantly, however, outdoor kennels should be 'lockable' – there are plenty of unscrupulous people ready and willing to steal and sell a well-trained, useful dog.

CCTV, security lighting and sensors are also a good idea – as is a free-roaming guard dog of the right sort!

Alarming figures

Gun dog owners of years ago didn't have the advantage of CCTV options around their premises, outbuildings and dog kennels – but then again perhaps there was not the same need as it was, for instance, virtually unheard of for anyone to steal a keeper's dog.

Not so nowadays and the sporting press, sadly, all too often contains reports of gun dogs being stolen. Generally, it seems that more than 5,000 dogs have been reported stolen to police forces in England and Wales since the beginning of 2013 – a startling 22.6 per cent rise in two years.

POO-PICKING PINEAPPLE PREVENTION

And finally – as they say at the end of many a news broadcast – some dogs, for reasons only known to themselves, seem to have an unpleasant habit of eating their own poo. Those far wiser than I claim that, if you give your dog pineapple (chunks or slices appear not to matter) in its daily diet, there's something in the pineapple that once digested, taints the animal's faeces in such a way that they are no longer tempted into feasting on their own body waste. Fact or fiction, I couldn't possibly say ... now, if anyone can give me a definitive answer as to how best to prevent a dog from rolling in fox excrement, in that I would be interested!

Bibliography, Further Reading, References and Sources

Barraud, E. M.: *Tail Corn*; Chapman & Hall, 1948.

Birkhead, T.: *Do birds smell?*; (available as a website download), British Trust for Ornithology, 2012.

Cassell, Jay & Fiduccia, Peter: *The Little Red Book of Hunter's Wisdom*; Skyhorse Publishing, 2011.

Common, James: *A Summer on a Scottish Grouse Moor*; www.wildlifearticles.co.uk, November 2015.

Countryman's Weekly: various articles published in my weekly column 2005–17.

Coward, Thomas: *Crowing pheasants and the North Sea Battle* – article originally published in *The Manchester Guardian*, February 1915, but reproduced in the 'Environment' section of *The Guardian*, 8 February 2015.

Daniels, Cora Linn & Stevans, C. M. (editors): *Encyclopaedia of Superstitions, Folklore, and the Occult Science of the World* – *volume II* (originally published in 1903); University Press of the Pacific, 2003.

Easyfrenchmontpellier.com: *Friday 13th in France* online article published 13 November 2015.

Fieldsports: various articles published 2016.

Field, The: various articles published 1853–present day.

Gilbertson & Page: *A Gamekeeper's Handbook*; Gilbertson & Page, 1954.

Gilbertson & Page: *The Control of Vermin*; Gilbertson & Page, 1938.

Gladstone, Hugh S.: *Record Bags and Shooting Records*; H. F. & G. Witherby, 1922.

Grahame, Kenneth: *The Wind in the Willows*; Methuen, 1908.

Greener, W. W.: *Gunnery in 1858: being a treatise on Rifles, Cannon, and Sporting Arms, explaining the principles of the science of Gunnery, and describing the newest improvements*; Smith, Elder & Co., 1858.

Greener, W. W.: *The Gun and its Development*; (9th edition), Crown, 1910.

Griffiths, Sarah: *Counting Crows! – Daily Mail* online article published 10 June 2015.

Harris Tweed Authority, The: website homepage and blog.

Hare, C. E.: *The Language of Field Sports*; Country Life, 1939.

Hastings, Macdonald (editor): *Country Fair*; Prion (an imprint of the Carlton Publishing Group), 2007.

Henniker-Heaton, Rose: *The Perfect Hostess*; Methuen & Co. Ltd, 1931.

Hobson, J. C. Jeremy: *A Practical Guide to Modern Gamekeeping*; How To Books, 2012. Hobson, J. C. Jeremy: *Beagling*; David & Charles, 1987.

Hobson, J. C. Jeremy: *The Shoot Lunch*; Quiller Publishing, 2011.

Hobson, J. C. Jeremy & Jones, David S. D.: *Sporting Lodges: Sanctuaries, Havens and Retreats*; Quiller Publishing, 2013.

Holt, Peter: *The Keen Countryman's Miscellany*; Quiller Publishing, 2012.

Home Office, the: *Guide on Firearms Licensing Law*; (available as a PDF download) UK Government, 2015.

Hutchinson, Horace (ed): *Shooting (volumes 1 & 2)*; Country Life, 1903.

Ingersoll, Ernest: *Birds in Legend, Fable and Folklore*; Longmans, Green & Co., 1923.

Jarman, Robert: *Shooting and the Etiquette*; The Gentleman's Journal (online), *www.thegentlemansjournal.com*, 2012.

Jones, David S. D.: *Gamekeeping: An Illustrated History*; Quiller Publishing, 2014.

Jones, Owen & Woodward, Marcus: *A Gamekeeper's Notebook*; E. Arnold, 1910.

Little, Carolyn: *The Game Cook*; Crowood Press, 1998.

Lovegrove, Roger: *Silent Fields: The long decline of a nation's wildlife*; Oxford University Press, 2008.

Marriat-Ferguson, J. E: *Visiting Home*. Published privately, 1905.

Merck: *The Merck Manual of Pet Health*; Merck, digital edition, 2014.

NFU: *Countryside (food, farming and rural life)* magazine; March, 2016.

Oliver, Harry: *Black Cats & April Fools — origins of old wives tales and superstitions in our daily lives*; Metro, 2009.

Page, Robin: *Weather Forecasting: The Country Way*; Penguin Books, 1977.

Pollard, Hugh B. C.: *Game Birds and Game Bird Shooting*; Eyre and Spottiswoode, 1936

Proud, Steve: *The Penguin Guide to the Superstitions of Britain and Ireland*; Penguin, 2006.

Sedgwick, Noel M.: *With Dog and Gun*; Herbert Jenkins, 1951.

Shooting Gazette, The: various articles published between 1999 and the present day.

Taylor, Leighton: *26 knife superstitions you probably didn't know*; *www.survivalknifeexpert* blog, May 2015.

Thomas, Gough: *Shooting Facts and Fancies*; A. & C. Black, 1978.

Wallop, Harry: *What your wellies say about you*; online *Daily Telegraph* article published 1 September 2015.

White, Gilbert: *The Natural History and Antiquities of Selborne*; Benjamin White, 1789.

Wilkins, John: *The Autobiography of an English Gamekeeper*; T. Fisher Unwin, 1892.

www.gunsonpegs.com/shooting/blogs/shooting-superstitions_2295; November 2015.

Young, Toby: *The Myths of the English Countryside*; online *Spectator* article published August, 2013.